PEOPLE
LEADERSHIP

PEOPLE LEADERSHIP

 Proven Strategies
to Ensure Your
Team's Success

Gina Folk

SHE WRITES PRESS

Published 2015
Printed in the United States of America
ISBN: 978-1-63152-915-3
Library of Congress Control Number: 2014955315

For information, address:
She Writes Press
1563 Solano Ave #546
Berkeley, CA 94707

This book is dedicated to my family. No matter what dream I've shared or action I've taken, you have been there with me every step of the way, reminding me that I can do anything, no matter how big the challenge. Mom, Dad, Chad, Kady, Sofia, Conner, Kat, Joe, and Kevin, your love for me is never questioned, and I am blessed to have you in my life. Nanny, Poppy, and Grandmother, although you are with me in spirit now, your love and guidance throughout my life made me feel like I was the smartest, prettiest, and most successful person in the world. I miss you very much and cherish the times we had together.

"In the end, all business operations can be reduced to three words:
people, product, and profits. Unless you've got a good team, you can't do much with the other two."

—Lee Iacocca

Contents

Introduction

In late 2009, I was playing with the idea of starting my own business— searching for something to do besides work in corporate America—when I received a marketing e-mail promoting a webinar on how to make millions on the college speaking circuit. I love to travel, I enjoy speaking, and the concept of teaching others and making money on my own time and terms felt good to me, so I signed up.

The day of the webinar came, and one of the first things the person hosting the call said was that the number one thing you can do to boost your ability to make money on the college speaking tour is to write a book. Not just any book, though—it has to be a book on a subject college professionals are interested in. Of the various hot topics the speaker mentioned, leadership was one of the top five. *I know about leadership*, I thought. I've been a leader of many teams and organizations, and I've learned a lot of valuable lessons over the years. I immediately talked myself out of that idea, however, convinced that because I wasn't a CEO or in the executive suite, I wasn't qualified to write a book on leadership.

So I tried to put that idea aside. But no matter what I did, I kept hearing this nagging voice in my head saying, "Gina, you need to write a book on leadership." Every time that thought popped up, I dismissed it—but I also started reading and rereading every book I could find on leadership. I wanted to see what the experts were saying, and I wanted to see what made these writers "experts" on the subject of leadership. And as I scoured those books, I realized two very important things: 1) Almost every single book was about making the reader a better leader for him or herself personally and not for the benefit of the people, teams, or organizations he or she leads; and 2) Most of the authors were sharing theories and best practices, but very few of them had actual hands-on experience with leading people.

With this information under my belt, I finally convinced myself that I was just as much of an expert as these published authors were on the subject of leadership—in fact, I felt that I had what many of them did not have: a love of leading others and actual experience in doing it. I was not a management consultant, and I didn't hold a doctorate of anything, but I was—and am—a true-blue, hands-on manager with years of real experiences, good and bad, in leading people and organizations under my belt.

The leadership advice I have to offer I learned over the course of twenty-plus years in different departments and teams at Nortel, a Fortune 500 telecommunications company that met its unfortunate demise when it filed for bankruptcy in early 2009. In those twenty-plus years, I was promoted from an individual contributor to a manager of a small group to a director with 300 people working under me. My leadership experience crossed over different groups and types of workers, including both white-collar and blue-collar organizations.

Like many of my peers, I began my career thinking that being a leader was all about my personal results. I worked diligently and strategically to be the best at every goal and objective I was assigned, and I was a good employee. But because I was so focused on my personal success, I spent the first five years of my career overlooking the importance of my team. With each promotion came more responsibility, however, and as I climbed the corporate ladder, I quickly realized that my personal performance could not be my sole form of success. Through trial, error, and humbling learning experiences, I discovered that being a good leader was about encouraging and empowering my team members to be successful. I made a ton of mistakes throughout my years as a leader—but I learned from every single one of them. My team members taught me which leadership tactics worked and which ones didn't, and the more I grew into being a people leader instead of a self-interested leader, the more my efforts *and* my team's efforts were recognized. I received numerous leadership and excellence awards from the executives at Nortel—but more importantly, by the time I was a director there, I had people begging to work on my teams. I didn't just study leadership; I lived it.

The moment the seed of the idea for this book was planted, I began taking notice of the number of articles and blogs that were appearing about how unhappy with their jobs workers in U.S. businesses are. In late 2013, the Gallup Organization interviewed nearly 150,000 workers across industries in the United States and discovered that more than 70 percent of the American workforce is either not engaged or completely disengaged from their jobs. This means people are not showing up for work at all, or, when they are at work, they are only going through the motions. Gallup noted that one of the main drivers of a person's engagement level is the effectiveness of the person's immediate supervisor. There it was in black and white: the validation I needed. Good leadership is vital to an individual's performance and, by extension, an organization's bottom-line results.

I wrote this book to offer guidance to anyone who leads people on a daily or frequent basis. Whether you're a business owner, CEO, supervisor, manager, project team leader, teacher, or even parent, it is my hope that this book can inspire you to be a more effective people leader.

What to Expect from This Book

Throughout my career, I frequently heard managers say that the worst part of their job is leading people. If you are a manager, team leader, supervisor, or even executive, you most likely achieved that position because of your individual performance results and accomplishments. Being promoted to leadership was probably your reward for a job well done. If you are like most people in leadership, however, you received very little if any guidance on what to do once you had people working for you. Getting results by way of others is very different than controlling your own actions and outcomes—and a lot of leaders get tripped up by that difference.

If you are one of these leaders, this book is intended to serve as a tool that you can use every day to give you that one piece of advice you may need in order to get your team members more engaged or performing more effectively. Chapter by chapter, this book offers the thirty most impactful and effective techniques I used throughout my own career and which I now pass on to the companies I work with. My hope is that you will read them and try them out yourself. We all have a leader inside of us—but it takes desire, guidance, and practice to perfect that persona. If you embrace and try these techniques, I can guarantee that you and your team will receive amazing results from your efforts.

You do not have to read this book in order; no one topic is more important than another, and I wrote it so that you could open it up on any day, at any time, and get the pearl of wisdom you need to lead your people in that moment. It's laid out in thirty short chapters. (I kept them short on purpose; I understand how harried your workday is. This book is designed for you to keep at your desk, and you can read a chapter when you need it in less than ten minutes!) Each chapter includes key points about a given leadership tip, a story representing the tip in action, and a thinking exercise for you to complete on your own time. All the stories are from my days at Nortel, though people's names have been changed to protect their identities.

I encourage you to read this book with an open mind. Some of these tips may work well for you and others may not; you don't have to adopt all of them. But each of the techniques I've covered here enabled me to turn low-performing teams into high-performing teams—to keep each and every one of my team members engaged and extremely effective in their performance results—so they're all worth a try.

I encourage you to practice and refine these techniques to suit your personality and your company's culture.

I also encourage you to seek support in this process, whether from a mentor, a coach, or your colleagues. Being a people leader can be a very lonely role; you may feel like you have the weight of the world on your shoulders and nowhere to turn to for guidance or advice. Find someone—within your company or outside it—whom you can share your burden with. In fact, if you like what you read (And I'm sure you will!), *I* would love to work with you—as long as you have the desire and are willing to invest in being a more effective people leader. If you are interested, you can find more about how to contact me in the back of this book.

My last piece of advice on how to read this book is simple but important: Have fun with it!

1

Be Authentically Transparent

The business world is known for trendy leadership practices and buzz-words. In the late 1990s, the word du jour was "transparency." The intent behind the principle was that leaders would communicate openly and with clarity. The expectation was that they would share with their teams everything they knew about business plans and conditions. In reality, what happened was that leaders would hold meetings or conference calls with their team and share some filtered information, and later the employees would find out from another department or another leader that important details had been withheld from them.

This continued to happen again and again, and over time, employees began to expect that when leaders said they were being transparent, they meant just the opposite—that they were not being authentic or truthful. Their BS meters kicked into gear; they heard the warning bells going off, saying, "Watch out for what comes next, because it's only going to be *part* of the story"; and their guard went up. And they didn't believe a word they heard.

That's why this chapter focuses on being *authentically* transparent. When you communicate with authentic transparency, you disclose everything. There are no hidden agendas or underlying assumptions. You place your trust in your team—and in turn, they place their trust in you.

You can achieve this level of transparency by:
- Letting others know who you are and what makes you tick.
- Communicating openly and candidly.
- Disclosing how and why you make key business decisions.
- Being consistent.

Share who are you and what makes you tick.

Letting your team know who you are—informing them about your personal and professional values, preferred leadership and communication style, strengths and gaps, what motivates you to achieve, and what is fun to you—establishes a personal connection, and it demonstrates that you have a good grasp of what drives you personally and professionally. It shows your team that you are human just like them, and it puts a strong foundation in place on which trust and respect can be built. If your team does not know you, they will be unsure of your motives—and they will be hesitant to give you their best performance.

Communicate openly and candidly.

Transparency requires being direct in your communications. Bottom line: no hidden agendas. This means sharing details about important business decisions without sugarcoating or watering them down, and it means reporting on the facts, regardless of whether the news is good or bad. People can see right through half-truths, so it is best to avoid them. If you have confidential information that cannot be shared for some reason, tell your team that. It is very easy—and entirely acceptable—to say, "I cannot share this news with you right now as it is confidential. I will share it with you as soon as possible." But whenever you can share information, do; the better informed your team is, the less likely they will be to waste their time and energy on gossip and water-cooler speculation.

Disclose why you make the key business decisions you make.

Offering your team insight into how you make decisions enables them to both understand your thinking process and to learn from it. When your team members know and understand your decision-making process, they can learn to "think like you"—and that means that they will be better equipped to make decisions on their own in the future that will be in alignment with your expectations. The better your employees become at making decisions on their own, the more time and money you and your organization will save.

Be consistent.

Your transparency must be consistent. If you are open and candid in some situations and not others, your behaviors will cause confusion in your group. Inconsistency sends a message that you are wishy-washy and are not certain of yourself. When you leave your team wondering which side of the fence you are going to be on today, they also wonder how much they can trust and respect you and your abilities as their leader. Demonstrating your consistency, in contrast, especially when sensitive events and situations occur, will solidify their confidence in you and in themselves. This confidence will allow them to perform at their best instead of wasting energy wondering what the "real" story behind the story is and how it will affect them.

Authentic Transparency in Action

My former company, Nortel, participated in a significant number of mergers and acquisitions while I was there. Because of my role at that time, I was often informed of the deals before they were made public—but due to the sensitive nature of these transactions, I had to operate under a nondisclosure agreement (NDA). This meant I could not share any information with anyone who was not under the same agreement.

The first time that I was involved in one of these projects, I wanted to be authentically transparent with my team from the very beginning. We had participated in these types of projects before, and one of our big frustrations in the past had been that we never received much information about them. Sometimes we would hear about them through the grapevine; other times, the executive in charge of the program would send an e-mail to tell us that he or she was working on a top-secret project but would then offer no other information. In both cases, speculation ran rampant. More often than not, the information being spread around was incorrect, and we wasted a lot of time and energy wondering and worrying about the impact these programs would have on us. As an employee, this behavior drove me nuts. I abhor gossip, and yet I frequently found myself getting just as hypnotized by rumors as everyone else. I always wondered why our bosses did not come down the hall or hold a call and tell us what they could without violating the NDA so that we could dispel at least some of the lies coming through the rumor mill. I was sure there was information they could give us to prevent us from trying to piece it all together ourselves. I was determined to do things differently if I were ever on a sensitive project.

So, when my time came to be under the NDA, I held true to my decision. Immediately after signing the NDA, I held a conference call with my team. I informed them that I had just been assigned to my first sensitive project, that my time would be focused on this program, and that I would be fairly inaccessible until it was done. I told them I wanted them to know that I was not evading them or trying to hide anything from them; then I gave them a high-level overview of the program and the projected timeline, explaining to them that I could not provide any details because I was under a nondisclosure agreement. I cautioned them to be mindful of the wildfire of gossip that projects like these instigate, and I assured them I would keep them up-to-date with the specifics as I could. Although their curiosity was piqued, my team appreciated my honesty and expressed their support to help in the project when the time came.

A few days after our meeting, I got a call from one of my team members, Janet. She told me she had just talked to Grace, a woman in another department, and Grace was freaking out because she'd heard the project that was in the works was going to eliminate all of their jobs. Janet said she told Grace that I was working on the project and that she trusted that I would tell them any details when I could—and that she tried to reassure her that what she was hearing was just a rumor, and to not believe everything she heard through the grapevine. Then she asked me if there was anything else that I could share.

Because I was legally bound not to share any information about the project at that time, I reminded Janet that I could not answer her question, but I assured her that any facts I learned would be shared with the team as I received them over the next few weeks. I encouraged Janet to continue to focus her thoughts and energy on her current role and responsibilities instead of group speculation. Although I could not relieve her concerns 100 percent, Janet knew that I had been as open and honest as I could be under the circumstances, and she thanked me for that.

After the call, I cringed. The rumor mill in action again. But I was happy that I had shared with my team what I could, and I felt comfortable that I had been authentically transparent.

A few weeks later, after the nondisclosure agreement was lifted, I provided my team with the full details of the project. When they learned that the program was actually going to provide *more* job security for everyone—not eliminate jobs, as Grace had heard—it was an eye-opener for some, I'm sure, about how unreliable gossip can be.

Going forward, each time we had a nondisclosure project, I openly communicated my role on the project and delivered the details as soon as they were available. There was always some nervousness in the air in the weeks before I was able to say more, but my transparency allowed my team to focus on their own work and not on the gossip.

People Leadership Action Steps to Being Authentically Transparent

1. Reflect on your ability to be transparent with your team. Would your team agree with your assessment?

2. What actions can you take to be more authentically transparent with your team?

3. Think about a time you witnessed transparency in leadership. How was it executed, and what were the results?

"In the end, I've found, people like the direct approach. It's much more valuable to them to have a leader who's absolutely clear and open than to have one who soft-soaps or talks in circles.

—Bill Parcells

2

Be Adaptable

It's a truism that no two people are alike, and that's especially important to remember when you're leading people. We all have different personalities and values. The manner in which we do our best work, and the pace at which we do it, varies from person to person. Each of us has our own work ethics and standards, as well as our own motivations; individuals on your team are not robots or minions. That's why people leaders are most effective when they are adaptable to their team's needs. Many managers and leaders expect their teams to adjust to their style; however, in projecting this expectation, they actually shut out their employees' ability to personally express themselves, which stifles their performance and productivity. Similar to the chameleon that adapts its colors to blend in with its surroundings, people leaders needs to adjust their style to benefit their teams.

Being adaptable means:

- Understanding and valuing each team member's individuality.
- Determining what each person on your team expects from you.
- Changing your approach to produce mutually beneficial results for each person or situation.

Make efforts to understand and value each team member's individuality.

Understanding each person's individuality starts with an interactive conversation. In our very busy world, people have a lot more going on in their lives than what they feel comfortable revealing on the surface. Take a few minutes of your time to discover more about each team member's individual circumstances. Find out about their families and how they like to spend their time after work. Listen to all the activities they have outside of their jobs, and think about how you can contribute in a positive way to the balance between their work and their personal lives. Ask them about the personal values that drive how they make decisions and live their lives. Discover what motivates them to achieve their highest potential. Find out why their jobs are important to them. Are they in it for the paychecks to support their families, or is it important to them that they use their talents for positive impact? Inquire about their career aspirations: do they strive to be leaders, or are they quite happy being worker bees? Get a sense of their work ethic: are they self-starters, or do they need more encouragement and direction? Uncover their perceptions of their personal strengths and what they enjoy most about their jobs. Allow them to freely share about any areas in which they would like to grow and develop.

Having personal and empathetic conversations with your team members not only allows you to get to know them; it can also provide you with some insight into yourself. Do not overlook the power that this personal connection can have for you and your organization. When made authentically, it shows your team members that you care about and value them as real people, not as commodities. Caring about others creates a strong foundation for trust; trust makes your employees feel valued; and employees who feel valued are highly innovative and productive.

Find out what your team expects of you.

In addition to getting to know your team members on an individual basis, it's helpful to understand the expectations that they have of you as their leader. This means allowing them to share the type of management support they need from you: Do they do better with a lot or a little direction and guidance? How do they like to receive feedback? Is it important for them to talk to you every day, or can you touch base less frequently? Do they communicate best over the phone or through e-mail, or do they need an occasional face-to-face visit?

Uncovering a team's expectations is an area where many leaders feel uncomfortable. With their own work plate full of deadlines and tasks, many leaders feel like they do not have the time or the patience to tailor their communications to each individual employee. I had that same mind-set at one point in my career. Actually, I was worse: I expected my team to watch the way I operated, read my mind, and perform their work in a way that met my high standards. What that translated into in reality was that my employees were extremely unsure of themselves, so they included me on every thought they had, every decision they wanted to make, and every action they planned to take. Their need for my attention and time was overwhelming.

When I finally got frustrated with these operating conditions, I reached out to each one of my team members to come up with a more effective way of working together. What I discovered was that a common agreement on how best to work together resulted in much less work for me and for them. Although it took a little more time up-front on my part to be proactive in understanding their needs, it was completely worth it in the long run.

Change your approach when the situation calls for it.

Once you have an idea of what your team members expect from you, adapt your style, and apply it to meet their needs—and if an employee asks for something you cannot deliver, negotiate an alternative. At first this may not feel easy or worth your time and effort. It can sometimes feel like it would be more productive for your team to adapt to you and *your* needs, and not the other way around. You are the boss, after all, right?

Whatever your reservations, I can assure you that you will ultimately waste more of everyone's time if you expect your team members to do everything your way. Why? Because they will always be second-guessing whether they are doing the right thing. Some employees will actually become almost paralyzed and afraid to act; others will spend all their time complaining about what a terrible boss you are and how impossible you are to please. And neither of these states of being is effective or productive for your employees or your company.

Proactively adapting to your mutually agreed-upon plan, in contrast, demonstrates that you value each of your employee's input, individuality, and needs. It allows them to feel heard and appreciated, and from your perspective, if you think about it, it's actually the ultimate form of control, because it allows you to create more focused and directed communication and expectations.

Adaptability in Action

About eight years into my career came one of my hardest and best lessons about leadership adaptability: I was promoted into the position of Director of Distribution, which made me responsible for the day-to-day operations of three large warehouses across the country. Up until this time, I had only led teams of white-collar workers, mainly in customer service—an environment far different from the warehouse floor—and I was one of the youngest female executives in the division.

I remember the first day I walked into our largest warehouse. I entered the building dressed in a nice business suit and high-heeled shoes—not exactly "warehouse attire"—trying as hard as possible to project confidence and competency. It didn't matter to me that I had never worked in, or even been in, a warehouse up until that time. I was convinced that my job was to show these workers a better way to operate.

In my first all-hands meeting with my employees, I shared my ideas on how things were going to change now that I was in charge. I assured them that if they followed my advice, we would be the best-performing warehouse in the company. As I rambled on confidently about my expectations and leadership style, I could see that some of them were shaking their heads in disbelief, while others were smirking, whispering to one another under their breath, and even rolling their eyes. I just kept moving through my speech, even though I could sense the discord in the room. After all, I was their fearless leader, and I had some great ideas about how to make things work better.

At the conclusion of the meeting, I felt like I had done a good job sharing my expectations, intentions, and excitement about my new role. Based on the reactions I saw in the employees, I knew I had some skeptics—but I was confident that over time they would come to see that my ideas would make the warehouse's operations run more smoothly. I had clearly communicated what I thought was being done wrong, what needed to change, and how that change needed to be effected. I had outlined an amazing plan for improvement, and now all my employees had to do was make it happen.

Because I felt that I had been so clear in my demands, I expected immediate improvements—but after a few weeks had passed, nothing had changed. Our daily performance reports provided evidence that results were actually getting worse, not better. When I questioned my supervisory staff about the situation, they assured me that change was happening and that all was well. But the numbers don't lie; I knew that something was off.

I decided it was time to go out to the floor and talk to my employees directly. Up until that time I had only been on the floor with a supervisor by my side; I hadn't gone out and actually had a one-on-one conversation with any of the workers. This time, instead of having the information be filtered or directed by my leadership team, I wanted to get firsthand information from the people in the trenches.

As I walked the floor, I could tell that a lot of people were intimidated by my presence and felt too uncomfortable to share their true thoughts with me. They were very cordial, but guarded. I received a lot of comments like "Everything is great—we're just happy to have jobs" or "We like your ideas—it just takes some time to change." Out of everyone I spoke to, only two team members, Katy and Jordan, were bold enough to voice their concerns. Katy, who was the first to offer her opinions, told me, "You may be good at what you did at corporate, but things work differently around here. Our jobs require hard work. We try to do a good job, but we don't get any support. The warehouse is the end of the road, and we get dumped on all the time. We're not appreciated for what we do—and no one tells us anything about why or how we are important to the company. If you want better results, why don't you try understanding us first?"

Jordan shared similar concerns with me. "People are different here," he told me. "They're doing real work—you know, work that requires physical activity, not just sitting at a desk in front of a computer and answering phones. You ought to take the time to get to know them before you try to change anything."

My ego did not like this input. I could feel myself getting defensive and frustrated; all I wanted to do was stomp my foot and yell, "If you would stop whining and just do what I say, things would be better around here!" My gut, however, was telling me to just listen to what they had to say. *You should listen to them*, said a tiny voice inside my head. *It took guts for them to speak up; the least you could do is honor that. Maybe you should provide a safe space for more people to talk to you.*

I spent several sleepless nights wrestling with my ego and my gut. Finally, I decided to at least try to listen. *It's not going to hurt anything*, I thought. *I'm the boss; if I don't like what I hear, we can still do it my way.*

After that personal awakening, I held a series of meetings with small groups of employees. I invited them to share about themselves; I inquired about what they were looking for in a leader, and what they needed from me and my supervisory team to make their work more productive and meaningful; and I encouraged each employee to share their fresh ideas about what we could change together to make the entire team more successful. As I listened to them open up and express their thoughts, I finally saw that I had been expecting them to adapt to my style—a style that worked in the corporate office environment but did not translate well to the warehouse environment. I was impressed with the courage they demonstrated as they expressed their concerns and the innovation they displayed as they shared their creative ideas.

In the weeks following those meetings, I began to adapt my style. My leadership team and I also began implementing some of the employees' ideas—and as we did that, we saw performance start to improve. More important, I saw people becoming happier and more fulfilled in their jobs. I watched the confidence in some of my employees soar—and that made me feel awesome and energized.

This was my first real lesson in adaptability. As a people leader, I finally understood that it was my responsibility to adapt to meet their needs. Transforming my style enabled us to work as a team to produce more effective and profitable results for our organization.

People Leadership Action Steps to Being Adaptable

1. List the ways in which you feel you are adaptable with your team. Would your team agree with your assessment?

2. What steps can you take to become more adaptable as a leader?

3. Describe a time when a boss adapted—or did not adapt—his or her style for you. How did it make you feel?

"As a leader you should always start with where people are before you try to take them to where you want them to go."

—Jim Rohn

3
Respect and Appreciate Diversity

What makes a painting beautiful? The subject? The focus? The style of the artist? The frame? The varying colors? The answer is *all of the above*. A beautiful picture is the result of a range of diverse qualities and characteristics; it's multidimensional. And so are people.

In today's world, as technology and globalization are making the physical boundaries of distance less and less restrictive, all of us are increasingly being exposed to different kinds of people. In both our personal and our professional interactions, we are almost guaranteed to come into contact with people different than us—people gifted with talents, beliefs, expressions, thoughts, and emotions unlike our own—and we must be comfortable interacting with those individuals. With the growing melting pot of people and personalities in the global workplace, diversity is something we must embrace—not only because it's the open-minded thing to do, but also because it is critical to our success.

In order to respect and appreciate diversity as a people leader, you must:

- Be well versed in all equal-opportunity laws, regulations, and guidelines.
- Recognize fears associated with differences.
- Let go of your fears and be curious.
- Leverage the differences for the greater good.

It's the law, ma'am!

As the workforce has diversified, local and federal governments have adopted a myriad of equal-opportunity laws to ensure fair treatment of all employees—laws that are designed to protect the rights of individuals of different genders, races, ages, sexual preferences, religions, physical abilities, and cultures. The first key in respecting diversity in your team is to familiarize yourself with your state's, country's, and organization's laws and policies. As a people leader, you must have a working knowledge of the equal-opportunity laws, regulations, and guidelines that are applicable to your business. If you are unaware or unsure of the laws, proactively reach out to a human resources or legal professional to educate yourself. You must be equipped with a strong understanding of these laws and then ensure that you adhere to them when dealing with your employees.

Effective people leadership doesn't stop with self-education, however; a good leader shares these diversity laws with their team members as well. Awareness of and adherence to equal-opportunity laws will empower you and your team to respect the legal aspects of diversity.

Acknowledge your fears.

Appreciating diversity requires recognizing our human tendency to be scared or threatened by people who don't look, think, and act like us. As with many animals, it's in our nature to hang out in packs of beings that are similar to us, and we tend to feel threatened when someone new comes in from the outside. It's an automatic response; we are innately fearful of anything or anyone that's unfamiliar to us. The brain actually turns on its fight-or-flight mechanism when it encounters unfamiliar circumstances or individuals.

Our "fight" response to the unknown encourages us to defend our territory and stand our ground. Just like a lion protecting his pride, our immediate response is to roar out at whatever is new or different in our surroundings. In order to feel safe, we stand our ground and become protective of our territory. We may become outspoken and initiate conflict to push our own ideas, viewpoints, and agendas. Dominating a situation in our need to be right and insisting on doing things our way can feel like the best way to create a safe place for ourselves.

On the flip side, our "flight" response whispers silently to us that the person or situation we are facing may be harmful or cause us discomfort, and it drives us to run away and refuse to associate with that potential threat. We go to our proverbial "corner of the ring" and hope the person or threat will move on to another place.

Think back to the last time someone had a unique idea or introduced a new way of doing something in your workplace. What was your immediate response? Was it one of excitement and curiosity? Or was it a feeling of fear and uncertainty? If you are like most people, your first reaction was probably a gut feeling that had you barking out, "We can't do it that way!" or "That just won't work!"—or that led you to simply remove yourself from the conversation and hope that it would go away. And how about when new people join your team? Are you open and welcoming to them? Or do you stay in your cubicle and hope you don't have to be "bothered" by them?

As a people leader, assess your feelings about diversity. Your team takes a lot of their cues on how to respond and act from your behavior, which means that if you are afraid of or feel threatened by diversity, they will mimic you. So if anyone on your team, including you, shows any signs of discomfort with or disrespect for someone else on your team or in your organization, address the issue. Don't ignore it and hope it will go away; diversity issues can fester and will magnify over time if they are not dealt with in a positive manner. Work with your team to help them understand that it is natural to feel threatened by differences, but that such feelings can be worked through and transformed into appreciation for the richness that diversity can bring to the table.

Get curious.

We all know the popular adage "Curiosity killed the cat." And if we think of the "cat" in this phrase as fear of the new and different, it's true! Curiosity is a very effective way to overcome fears of dissimilarity and diversity. Encourage each of your team members to play the role of a child in wonder (and make sure you try it as well).

One of the best ways to do this is to ask questions. Getting more educated about the facts tends to tone down our emotional reactions. It is always best to frame your questions in the form of how, what, where, or when. Avoid asking "why" questions; "whys" put all of us quickly on the defensive. Instead, ask things like "How do you see your idea benefitting the team?" or "What are your reasons for wanting to do that activity?"—and be genuinely interested in the responses to your questions. There is nothing worse than being asked a question and then feeling that the questioner is just going through the motions. Listen with interest and excitement instead of fear, doubt, or indifference. You may find amazing similarities in the people and situations you perceived as being so very different. Kill those personal fears of others by being curious!

Use differences to bring your team closer together.

Being equipped with a better understanding of diversity enables you to leverage the best qualities of each person. Think of each difference as a piece of a puzzle. When you first start working on a puzzle, all you see is a pile of pieces that appear to have nothing in common. As you take a better look at their distinct qualities, however, you begin to see patterns—and in order to complete the big picture, you must find how each of them works together. Think of your team members this way. Leverage their differences for the greater good of your organization.

There is an amazing richness in our personal differences when you're willing to open yourself up to it. The more we respect and appreciate the diversity in our midst, the better we are at collectively creating more effective and creative solutions, processes, and performance results.

Respecting and Appreciating Diversity in Action

As a project manager of numerous global programs, I encountered diversity all of the time. Our teams were made up of people from Singapore, Ireland, Australia, Canada, and the United States. We had a mix of men and women from various age groups and generations. Everyone had their own style of communication, including language, and we all had distinct personal and professional views.

I was assigned my first global project about twelve years into my career at Nortel. Up until that time, my team and I had successfully implemented projects across various U.S. states. With that experience under my belt, I entered the global program with a confident—bordering on arrogant—attitude. I expected that my counterparts from other countries would simply adapt to our style since we'd gotten such great results on prior projects. It did not take very long for humility to displace my confidence, however.

I will never forget our first call with the overseas team. Because we had a mix of European and Asian organizations, the vast array of languages and accents proved to be a challenge. It was difficult to follow along; I didn't always understand the meaning behind some of my new team members' words and expressions, and I found myself repeating, "I'm sorry, what did you say?" throughout our first series of phone calls. I felt especially ignorant because most of them could understand everything I was saying. They were much more educated about the United States than I was about their countries. Most of them had been to the States, whereas I had never left the country. I had no understanding of or appreciation for their countries and cultures, other than what little I remembered from my schooling or had seen on TV. I knew nothing about their living conditions or what their work environments were like.

I quickly became aware that there was much I didn't know about the people I was working with on this project; still, the business facts indicated that our market had the largest revenue, volume of orders, and biggest customer base, so I persisted in trying to run it as if it were a North American project. "The objective of this team is to create a process that meets our global markets' needs and that is based on doing business the way we do here in the States," I remember stating very boldly during one early call. I should have realized that the silence that greeted my assertion was not a sign that the rest of the team was in agreement with my opinions. Instead, in my ignorance, I continued leading the team through a series of calls about our current U.S. processes and market requirements, and whenever anyone highlighted customer requirements or process needs that were different from those in the States, I basically shut him or her down, declaring that the overseas team members would just have to adjust to "our" way of doing business. Looking back, I realize that I was simply uninterested in—and a little bit scared of—changing the way we did things.

We spent a few weeks marching down this path, and as time went on, I noticed participation starting to drop off. Team members missed meetings and critical deadlines. When they did show up for meetings, they remained silent, offering no input or updates. No progress was being made on this project, which was being closely watched by our executive team. I was disappointed and frustrated, but didn't know to what extent these results had been precipitated by my style of doing things.

In a moment of desperation, I threatened the overseas team members with consequences for their lack of participation and support. Their response was, "We will start participating when you take the time to understand our differences." Yikes!

After that big helping of humble pie, we "restarted" the project, this time allowing each person to reiterate his or her unique needs and processes. This time, I worked hard to understand the purpose and the benefit of each unique requirement posed by my overseas team members. Perhaps not surprisingly, as I learned about my team, I discovered we had a lot in common. Personally, we learned that some of us liked the same music, shared similar family situations, and enjoyed similar hobbies and fun activities. Professionally, we discovered that, regardless of our differences, all we really wanted was the most effective solution for our customers. Understanding our differences and commonalities allowed us to drop our defenses and collectively leverage the best ideas and practices from the group.

Once I was able to appreciate what my team members' different cultures and ways of operating brought to the table, we successfully designed a global process that delivered outstanding results—and we learned a lot about each other while we were at it, which was extremely fun and rewarding.

People Leadership Action Steps to Respecting and Appreciating Diversity

1. Describe the diversity in your current team.

2. How can diversity be used to make your team and organization more effective?

3. Describe a situation you've experienced where diversity was not accepted. How did it make you feel?

"Diversity: the art of thinking independently together."

—Malcolm Stevenson Forbes

4
Build a Strengths-based Team

To optimize performance on any team, good people leaders know they must create from a position of strength. To use a parallel from the sports world, can you imagine putting a star quarterback in a defensive back position? The team would have a tough time winning because even though that player is great at throwing a football, he probably won't be nearly as good at making the important tackles. The other defensive team members would be angry and frustrated that they have to play harder to offset his weaknesses. The fans would be upset because their team would likely be getting tromped by their competition. And the poor quarterback would feel deflated because even his best efforts would be ineffective and unappreciated.

A winning coach would never put any player in a position that does not leverage his or her talents and strengths—yet in the workplace, this is a very common practice. Many employees are assigned roles and given responsibilities that do not align with their strong qualities and skills. Just as in our football example, this practice produces poor results for your organization and creates unnecessary stress for individuals and their team members. If you want the most productivity from any group, it is best to create from a position of strength—not weakness.

Building a strengths-based team requires a proactive effort to:
- Define the success criteria for every role and objective.
- Define specific skill sets and behaviors required for each position.

- Assess each team member's strengths.
- Align the right people with the right work.

Figure out what success looks like.

Would you be able to create an effective map without having an idea of your final destination? Of course not! The same concept applies to building an effective team. You have to know what success looks like—you have to know what outcome(s) you want your team to achieve—in order to get there.

Is each job function or role within your team clearly defined? Are they documented and understood by the individuals in those positions? If not, what's preventing you from having discussions with your team and creating such documentation? In my experience, proactively defining and documenting the key desired accomplishments for each person you work with is the foundation for creating a strengths-based team. The end product provides a succinct and clear description of key success criteria for the function. With the outcome as your final destination, you can proceed with creating a detailed road map to success.

Identify the specifics.

With your success criteria in hand, develop a list of the needed skill sets and behaviors that are required to deliver the results. In many companies, the only place you see effort being made to define a job is on a job posting. Job postings are excellent examples of defining specifics, granted, but it is not effective to only create the specific requirement for your team when you need to hire a new person. If you want a team based on strengths, you must evaluate the role of each person you currently have on your team on a regular basis.

Be sure to create these definitions for the job and not for the person currently filling the role. If you are unsure of what is necessary for the job, ask your team members. After all, they are the ones that are closest to the details. Every function or major objective in your organization will benefit from documenting the specific needs required to meet your desired outcomes.

Assess your team members' strengths.

Understanding the specific aptitudes and talents of each of your team members enables you to better align the roles on your team with the people available to fill them. There are many tools that can be used to assess an individual's strengths. (In fact, you can find numerous assessments that will systematically reveal the key attributes that a person possesses simply by performing a quick online search.) My personal favorite assessment tool is *Strengths Finder 2.0,* a book created by Tom Rath and the Gallup Organization. When I took the free online test I gained access to when I bought the book, it quickly summarized my top five strengths, and they were very accurate—and I find the book itself extremely insightful. This is an easy and cost-effective way for you and your team to learn more about your personal strengths.

Another way to discover people's strengths is by asking them about themselves. The reactions you receive from your team members will vary. Some will quickly spout off a list of their talents and skill sets. Others will meet the question about their strengths with a "deer in the headlights" stare, or they will begin telling you about functions they do well. Most of us—myself included—find it very difficult to talk about ourselves! But regardless of the reaction you get, I encourage you to engage in this discussion with your people. Ask questions like "What tasks do you feel you perform effectively and efficiently?" "What current or past roles have made you energized at work?" "What do you feel most confident doing?" Asking these sorts of questions and listening to your team members' responses is a great way for you to learn more about your team, and for them to learn more about themselves, which will in turn help you ensure they are in roles in which they can feel motivated and perform effectively.

Align the right people with the right jobs.

Once you've gotten a better handle on the different strengths your team members are bringing to the table, it's time to play the match game; in other words, it's time to compare the required skills sets of each role with the strengths of the individuals on your team. Ask yourself, "Are my people in roles in which they can leverage their strengths?"

Many managers think they cannot afford to do this exercise because if they find any misalignment there will be nothing they can do about it. After all, they don't have the luxury of simply moving an individual to another job, do they? However, it is those same managers who complain about productivity and performance issues with their team members—because when people are in roles that don't leverage their individual talents, attendance, behavior, and/or performance problems begin to crop up. Doing a proper and thoughtful analysis and alignment of the roles available with the people best suited to them allows people leaders to easily assign the work to the people who will deliver maximum results.

There are several ways to align work to people's strengths. The extreme is that a person needs to change roles or leave the company. However, this is not always the case. There are instances in which you can help team members develop the strengths they need in order to thrive in their roles. Of course, this requires a willingness on your part to coach and train, and a willingness on the employees' part to actually grow. If that approach isn't an option, maybe you need to create a new position for an unfilled role and hire the needed skill set from the outside. You can also consider transferring the work to a team that is better suited to do the work; or, if your need is temporary and you know someone from a different department is just the element you need, ask to borrow that person until the project is finished. The bottom line is, as a people leader, it is your responsibility to ensure that you have the right person for the job—not only for the company, but also for the person. I can assure you that when you force an individual to do work (knowingly or unknowingly) in an area he or she is not suited for, no one will be happy with the outcome. It's like forcing a round peg into a square hole: no matter how hard you try to push it in, it will never be a good fit.

Developing high-performing teams and individuals requires building from their strengths first.

Strengths-based Teams in Action

Monica was the team leader of the System Support Department within a division of Nortel. In this role, her team was responsible for handling all questions, problems, and change requests for the system that was responsible for processing our customer orders for telephone hardware and software. Monica's team received over one hundred requests from customer service employees each day.

One month, Monica started receiving numerous calls about her team members' inadequacy in solving the users' issues or resolving their business needs. She was baffled. Her current team was comprised of extremely savvy individuals, programmers who were adept in writing and implementing coding for new features and reports. Whenever users located a system bug, the team quickly identified and corrected the issue. Monica knew they were some of the best technical people she had ever managed, and she couldn't understand why they were getting such negative reviews.

In an effort to defend her team, Monica performed an evaluation of the tickets that her team received, and she determined that over 75 percent of the requests her team was receiving were not technological questions or issues—they were process questions or requests for new user features to support the business. That explained the problem; her team members did not have the right skill sets or strengths to address the issues coming through on the tickets.

Upon discovering this, Monica went straight to her team, explained her findings, and let them know that in order to achieve maximum results, they needed to learn more about business process and how users were actually using their system. As she discussed this with her team, it became very clear that her programmers were best equipped to work with computers, not people. Monica knew she had a gap—so she discussed this concern with her manager, and they agreed that she needed to add someone skilled in business to her team. Monica interviewed customers and the director of her department in order to define what outcome the role needed to achieve, and with their input she formulated a detailed description of the traits and skills a person would need to possess in order to fill this role. The analysis showed that the job required someone well versed in the current customer ordering process who also demonstrated an aptitude with the technology of the customer order system.

After a series of internal interviews, Monica hired Alice. She had proven experience with customers and the order process, but what really made her stand out among her peers was her interest and initiative in learning from and working with the customer order system programmers. Alice also had strengths in both business and technology, which made her the perfect fit for the role. Within a month, the number of complaints and calls to Monica decreased dramatically, and the number of satisfied customer service representatives increased. Monica created a strengths-based team, and she got the results she was looking for.

People Leadership Action Steps to Building Strengths-based Teams

1. Assess each function in your organization. Do you understand the requirements for each role? Are your people aligned with the work best suited to their strengths?

2. What steps can you take to better align the work required to the strengths of the individuals on your team?

3. Think of a time when you knew your strengths were aligned properly with the position you were in. How was your performance in that role? How did you feel?

"The task of leadership is not to put greatness into people, but to elicit it, for the greatness is there already."

—John Buchan

5
Provide Clarity and Purpose

Imagine you're cruising down the road when all of a sudden a driving rain comes falling from the sky. As you urgently flip the switch to turn your windshield wipers on, you curse out loud at the realization that you still haven't gotten them replaced. They are so old and worn that they're not clearing off the rain landing on your windshield, and you can't see anything in front of you.

This has actually happened to me twice, and both times, I completely freaked out. I felt like I wasn't in of control of the car or what was going to happen to me. My father always told me to keep driving through heavy rain—"You never know when the rain is going to stop!"—but without working windshield wipers, I had two choices: pull over and wait out the storm, or keep driving and hope and pray that I would not hit anyone or anything on the road. That unclear windshield not only caused me anxiety; it also prevented me from moving forward to my destination in a clear and purposeful way.

This same kind of situation can happen with your team if they are unclear about the vision of your team or company. The people you work with need clarity and purpose: clarity because it provides individuals with a sense of control that enables them to be more productive and successful in their goals and everyday tasks; purpose because people are more motivated when they know why they're doing what they're doing. We all want to know that what we're doing is going to make some sort of impact.

As employees, we have a desire to know how we can contribute to the overall good of the company we work for. But what happens so often at work is that individuals are directed to perform a task in a certain way without being given the context of why they're doing it. I would venture to guess that if you surveyed one hundred people in your company and asked them why they perform one of their key tasks, eighty of them would say something like "Because we have always done it that way." And this is a problem, because going through the motions in any task or role will, at best, deliver mediocre results. We operate at our highest performance and motivation when we have a clear idea of where we are headed and when we understand how and why we contribute to the organization we're a part of.

People leaders offer clarity and purpose with:
- Mission and vision statements.
- Strategic planning.
- Individual performance objectives.

Mission = Purpose. Vision = Clarity.

Purpose is the "why" that drives our actions in life. It defines the reason behind and for the things we do. And just as important as the "why" is the "what," which provides clarity about the outcome we expect to achieve through our actions. In larger corporations, purpose is outlined in the company mission statement, and clarity is provided in the vision statement. In small- to medium-size organizations, mission and vision statements may only exist in the leader's head, if at all. No matter what size or type of organization you are a part of, however, it is critical for you and your team to understand your "why" and your "what." These two cornerstones serve as the foundation of your success. What would happen to a building that was built without a strong foundation? At some point, it would start to crack, shift, and eventually crumble to the ground, right? Well, the same thing can happen to your organization if your people do not have a strong understanding of its mission and vision.

There is a wealth of information out in the world today on how to effectively create mission and vision statements. Having created many of these over years for different departments and projects, I can tell you that there are three keys things to keep in mind as you come up with yours: 1) Keep them simple. Don't make them so verbose and elaborate that your employees and customers cannot understand them. 2) Make them descriptive. You want people to have enough detail so they can actually visualize the result you are describing. People need to be able to see the purpose or vision in order to move toward creating it. 3) Communicate them. Don't just let them be posted in the halls, on your website, or in your head; verbalize them on a regular basis. You want your team to act on them, and they can't do that if they aren't thinking about them.

Develop a strategy.

Strategic planning is often misunderstood. I have heard on more than one occasion from leaders in various companies and organizations, "I don't have the time or money to create a strategy. I just need my team to do the work and get results." But without a plan, how can you be assured you are approaching your outcome in the most effective manner, or that you will even reach your final destination? Your strategy is a high-level description of how you are going to meet your desired outcome. It defines the descriptive milestones that must be met in order to achieve your vision. Think of this plan as your company's high-level goals and objectives.

An effective strategic plan includes your top three to seven priorities for a given year, as well as the performance targets you expect to achieve. Ideally, you will complete the plan at the end of each fiscal year and share it with your entire team going into the beginning of the next one. When done properly, strategic planning will enable your team to have a clear picture of your desired destination.

Let people know how they can contribute.

Once they have a clear vision of where they're headed, your team members need to understand how they can help in the journey. Individuals are motivated to perform better when they understand how their actions will contribute to the outcome—and the best way to help them understand this is to create individual performance objectives that are aligned to the goals in the strategic plan.

I am not a big believer in the "SMART" (specific, measurable, achievable, realistic, and time-bound) goal-setting theory: it's too sterile, and it's too constrictive; people rarely follow the pattern, and because of that they end up setting goals that are not meaningful. Plus, this approach is not always applicable to key activities that are performed in business. That said, the most effective individual performance objectives are the ones that exist. You might be saying, "Well duh." To that I would respond, "Exactly"—but you would not believe how many people don't know what and how they are expected to perform over the course of a week, month, or year. They may have a basic understanding of the fact that they are expected to perform the duties of their jobs, but they have no compass for how they need to perform.

We crave knowing how we can best contribute. That's why it is so critical to provide each of your team members with goals and to convey to them your expectations of their performance as they strive toward those goals. Strong performance objectives have four qualities: 1) They are aligned to the company goals; 2) They provide enough description and detail that there is no room for doubt about what the desired outcome is; 3) They are designed to stretch your team members a little outside of their comfort zones, but not so much that they can't be successful; and 4) They need to be measurable, with either tangible dates that need to be met or performance targets that can be tracked. These objectives are twofold: they show your team members how they can contribute to the organization, and they define how their performance will be measured. People leaders should always make sure their employees have a crystal clear understanding as to how their performance contributes to the company's success. If you want people to perform at their best, they need to know they matter.

Providing Clarity and Purpose in Action

When Edgar was promoted to Director of North American Supply Chain Operations, he walked into a bit of an organizational mess. The previous director's leadership style had left the operations employees unmotivated and deflated. There was no clarity around the expectations or goals they were supposed to achieve. Edgar's predecessor had never shared the company's annual strategic plan and goals or given his employees personal performance objectives. As a result, the overall performance of the team had declined. Customers were constantly complaining about receiving their orders late. Employee absenteeism and turnover had increased. The team lacked direction, and they had lost their sense of purpose about their job.

About a week after Edgar started his new role, he began calling key employees in his organization in order to gather their thoughts about why the operation was struggling. He received comments like "We never knew what we were supposed to do" and "No one ever reached out to us to ask us for solutions; we just kept getting told to shape up or we would be fired." One of them told him, "After a while, we felt like we didn't matter, so why bother doing anything?" It was obvious to Edgar that the main problem with his department's performance was a lack of clear direction—so, with that information in mind, he scheduled a series of conference calls with his direct leadership team to outline the problem and create a plan for improvement.

At the first meeting, Edgar shared his perception that the department, as a whole, lacked clarity. His team agreed wholeheartedly with his diagnosis, and they told him they felt it was important for them to understand the overall company plan for the year. To make that happen, they spent the next series of meetings reviewing the company's strategic plan for the year and outlining how the operations organization could contribute to achieving those goals. From there, they created a departmental strategic plan with five primary goals and objectives, and then Edgar asked his leaders to create their own strategic plans for their teams.

After the completion of the plans, Edgar held a conference call with all one hundred employees in his group. In this call he reiterated the company's mission and vision; he shared the details of the company and the departmental strategic plans; and his leaders communicated the details of their team plans. After all the information was shared, he allowed the employees to ask questions. Once those questions had been addressed, Edgar explained that each of their leaders was going to work with them to create individual performance objectives based on these plans over the course of the next three weeks.

At the end of the three weeks, Edgar held a follow-up call with his leadership team to ensure they had completed their intended actions. He also checked in with his employees to make sure they were satisfied with the process. The reaction he received from these employees ranged from relief to excitement to gratitude. They felt that the leadership team was providing them the direction they needed to be successful. Soon afterward, Edgar's solution started to pay off. The internal metrics and performance results showed monthly improvements that, over the course of a year, led to best-in-class results for the company.

People Leadership Action Steps to Providing Clarity and Purpose

1. On a scale of 1 to 10, rate how effective your company's mission and vision statements are. What can you do to make them a 10?

2. Think about how your strategic plan, or lack thereof, has contributed to your organization's results. What could be done to make it more clear and purposeful?

3. Make sure each of your team members has individual goals and objectives and that each team member can clearly describe his or her purpose and how his or her actions impact your organization.

4. Think of a time when you clearly understood your purpose and the objectives of your position. How did that understanding impact your performance in that role?

"Good leaders make people feel that they're at the very heart of things, not at the periphery. Everyone feels that he or she makes a difference to the success of the organization. When that happens people feel centered, and that gives their work meaning."

—Warren G. Bennis

6
Delegate

People leadership requires delegation—assigning activities to other people. As simple as this sounds, relinquishing control to another is not easy. Perhaps we are concerned that the person in question does not have the skill set or is not reliable enough to take on the task; perhaps we believe that it will take longer to explain the work to someone else than it will to simply do it ourselves; perhaps we feel the activity has to be done a certain way and that no one is capable of achieving the results we can. As a leader, it's important that you understand that delegating is not about shifting the work from your plate to someone else's; it's a personal act of letting go of control and having faith in others.

In my experience, delegation requires:
- Having trust in your team's abilities.
- Setting clear expectations for the task.
- Letting go—and then following up.

Trust your team.
In order to let go and have faith, you must trust. Trusting your team members means having confidence in the ability of the person you're delegating to. That's a lot easier to do when you have individuals on your team who have the skill set, attitude, and proven performance record that is needed to effectively achieve the task at hand. Every person on your team is competent in something, or they would not be on your team. So when delegating,

choose the best person for the job that needs to be done. Strategically align the work to the right team member. Delegating in this manner empowers both you and the delegate: they are confident in their skill set, and you can rest assured that they will succeed in delivering the expected results.

Make your expectations clear.

Even the most capable person needs to have clear expectations in order to deliver effective results. Expectations provide a mutual understanding of what needs to be accomplished in any given task. With this in mind, before you hand off any work, create a written description of what success will look like after completion. This might include a narrative about the desired outcome and the working parameters for the job, or listing specific success criteria like deliverables, performance results, and timelines. Working parameters provide the person you're delegating to an idea of the decision-making authority they have, budget allotments for the task, and key process/system requirements or constraints. Keep in mind, though, that the expectations you set forth should not describe *how* something should be done—they should reflect what should be accomplished. When you trust your employees, you allow them to perform the tasks assigned them in the manner they see fit.

Let go—and follow up.

Relinquishing control and trusting in your team does not mean that follow-up is not required. Just the opposite is true, in fact; follow-up is essential in delegation. This does not mean, however, that you should nag your team members for hourly or daily status updates, and it doesn't mean that you should second-guess every detail and step they take toward their goals. Good follow-up is about consistent two-way communication. It works best when updates are provided on a regular and scheduled basis, though how the communication is done can vary depending on the task itself. Some projects lend themselves to e-mail updates, like status reports; others require more focused reviews in person or on conference calls. No matter which method you choose, make sure that both parties have agreed to it. It is very disheartening for an individual to produce reports that are never read and then to receive phone requests for the same information.

It's also disempowering for your employees to need your input and then not have a consistent way to reach out to you for guidance. Follow-up not only requires communication—it also requires support. If your team members encounter any roadblocks in the course of the project, you need to be there to help remove them.

The more you practice follow-up and receive consistent feedback, the easier it will be for you to let go. When done with trust, clear expectations, and follow-up, delegation produces outstanding results for both delegator and delegatee. Your team members will feel appreciated and motivated to do a stellar job—and you will free up your time so you can focus more on strategy and people leadership instead of day-to-day activities.

Delegation in Action

When Geraldine was appointed Senior Manager of Customer Service, it was because of her track record as an extraordinary customer service representative. The customers loved her; her peers in other departments, like sales and manufacturing, trusted her to answer tough questions and solve difficult problems within their groups.

When Geraldine moved into her new role, the director of operations reminded her that the new job required more team leadership and less involvement in the day-to-day activities with the customers. Geraldine assured her director that she understood and was excited to provide leadership to her team of customer service reps.

Several weeks went by, and Geraldine felt overwhelmed in her new role. She was spending a lot more hours on the job than she previously had. In fact, most days she was in the office earlier than her employees and left later than they did. Finally, during a regularly scheduled staff meeting with her team, Geraldine expressed her concerns. She shared with her team that she felt that she was doing all of their work, and she made a plea for them to help her come up with some solutions to relieve her workload—but she received nothing but silence from her employees.

Geraldine's people knew what the problem was, but they were hesitant to share it. The fact was that Geraldine was the issue. She had not let go of her old job. The woman she had hired and trained to replace her, Anne, had told her teammates more than once that her customers were contacting Geraldine directly—and that instead of referring them back to Anne, she was taking it upon herself to work with them to meet their needs. Anne had tried to share her frustrations with Geraldine, but she'd refused to accept the reality of the situation, and it was making it impossible for Anne to do her job.

As her overwhelm escalated, Geraldine went to her director and asked for his guidance. I was the process expert, so he delegated the problem to me.

My evaluation of the situation began with an in-depth, firsthand look at what was actually happening on a daily basis. This meant that I sat with each customer service representative, including Anne, and watched them work. After my first day of observation, it was crystal clear to me that a large part of Geraldine's issue was a lack of delegation. She was still doing her old job and was having a very difficult time letting go of the day-to-day interactions with her customers. Although she had hired Anne to take her place, she was still accepting calls directly from customers, and instead of bridging a relationship to Anne, she was talking them through everything herself. And she wasn't only doing this with her long-standing customers; she was doing it for all requests that came to her—requests that could easily be handled by someone else on her team.

I knew I had to relay my findings to Geraldine gently because she was convinced that her team members were the problem. So, in order to bring what was really happening to her attention, I sat down with Geraldine to review how she was spending her time on a daily basis. As she relayed what her day-to-day looked like, I could almost see the lightbulb go off in her head. She recognized that she was spending all of her time doing the detail work and none of her time supporting her team. Together we created an interim process: Each time Geraldine received a direct customer call, she would conference in the customer service representative responsible for the account, and collectively they would answer the customer's question. Over time, as she became more trusting of her team's competence, she was able to transfer the customer calls to the specific rep without listening in.

After a month of implementing this process, Geraldine was spending fewer hours at work and more of her time on the job leading her team. Anne and her peers, meanwhile, were very relieved and motivated by the knowledge that Geraldine was finally delegating the work to them.

People Leadership Action Steps to Delegating

1. Think about how you feel about delegating to your team.

2. Think about your current process for delegating. Are there any projects or tasks that you feel you cannot delegate? Why not?

3. Come up with some steps you can take to delegate more to your team.

4. Think of the most effective delegator you know. What makes him or her come to mind? What does he or she do differently than you?

"Surround yourself with the best people you can find, delegate authority, and don't interfere."

—Ronald Reagan

7

Communicate, Communicate, Communicate

Communication, in its purest form, is the exchange of information between two parties. The manner in which we receive and relay information to and from one another is a major contributor to the success of our actions and outcomes in life. We feel more competent and confident when we are well informed about situations and events in our lives. Our innate human nature craves to be "in the know" because having knowledge makes us feel special and important. Quite frankly, people are nosy. We like to know what is going on in and around our world. We've always been that way; that part of our nature doesn't change. *How* we communicate information, however, has changed dramatically, even in the past few years. Now more than ever people are addicted to an instantaneous connection to information. We live in a fast-paced information superhighway world that seems to be speeding up every day. Our most basic questions, like *Where should I go for dinner?* or *How do I find my destination?* can be answered within seconds on any smartphone, computer, or tablet.

This on-demand lifestyle has created an expectation of instant communication with people in our personal and professional lives. Smart phones have made us easily accessible to anyone, any time, anywhere, in a matter of minutes. We can connect quickly through text messages, e-mails, video chats, and voice conferences—and because this technology is always at our fingertips, we expect to be "in the know" and connected all the time. As people leaders, we must understand the changing dynamics of communication and how to make it work effectively for us.

In our world today, communication requires:

- Consistent and timely dissemination of important information.
- Content that is specific, relevant, factual, and truthful.
- Passion, energy, and authenticity.

Be consistent and timely.

In this world of instant facts and figures, it is critical now more than ever before to ensure that your communication to your organization is consistent and timely. One of the most frequent complaints I have heard from employees in business, volunteers in organizations, and even committee members of various groups is that the only way they receive important updates about their company or organization is through an external source or the internal grapevine.

People want and expect to hear important information from a trusted internal source—specifically, their leader. Lack of communication on your part is discouraging and deflating. When your team feels like they've been left out of the loop, time and productivity can be lost to inactivity due to fear of being uninformed, idle chit-chat and speculation about what team members think is happening, or the creation of team members' "stories" based on what they hear on the information superhighway. None of these ways of being is an effective use of time.

The best way to maximize productivity and communication is by sharing important information in a consistent and timely way. Remember, people can and will quickly find information when they want it—but most of us prefer to hear about the facts from someone we know and trust. If you are a leader in a publicly traded company, you may have some legal boundaries to consider in communication, like when and how you announce your financial information. However, don't let these boundaries prevent you from communicating at all. Share information with your internal team as often as you are able to. When companies just expect their employees to find information for themselves, it leads to one of two things: misinterpretation of the facts, or frustration about being kept in the dark.

If you are a small or privately held business, share important facts and figures with your team every month or quarter, not just once a year or not at all. And when you are presenting the details, do not give in to the temptation to filter the information. Don't be afraid to share the good news and the bad. Even when your team members don't like the news you're delivering, they will have greater respect for you as a leader knowing that you're honest about the good, the bad, and the ugly.

Consistent and timely communication is not just about finances and performance, by the way—it's about everything. When important decisions are made or new goals are created that impact the company, tell your team about them. Communicate quickly, and communicate all the time! It will minimize the time your team spends wondering and speculating about the state of the company, and it will make them feel like they are an important and valued part of your organization.

Be specific, relevant, factual, and truthful.

The "what" you share with your organization is just as important as the frequency with which it is shared. Make sure you create your message with your audience in mind. It is very tempting to simply forward news and fool yourself into thinking you're an excellent communicator; many leaders think, "If they want information, I'll show them information," and then they overwhelm their team with news that has no relevance or meaning to them. But giving content without the proper context and understanding of its impact on its recipients can be more damaging than not providing it at all. Doing this leaves too much room for personal interpretation and conjecture. People need to receive information in a form that makes sense to them. This means that when you share news with your team, you should frame it in a way that relates specifically to your people's role or function within your organization. Even the most basic details, like revenue and profitability numbers, need to be explained, because not everyone understands financial numbers and the meaning behind them. When you distribute information or instructions, whether written or verbal, include details that are both relevant and truthful. Nothing is worse than disclosing facts that don't matter or details that are only half-baked or half-truthful. When you communicate the facts, offer your opinions and interpretations, and clearly outline what is fact and what is personal thought on the matter at hand.

If, at any time, there is information you cannot share with your team, do not make something up or try to hide it. Simply tell them that you have confidential information that will be shared at a later date. Avoid any embodiment of the prison warden in the movie *Cool Hand Luke*, when he so arrogantly tells Luke and the other inmates, "What we've got here is a failure to communicate." Excel in your communication by being specific, relevant, factual, and truthful—and watch your team's performance do the same!

Speak passionately, energetically, and authentically.

We've discussed the when and the what, so now let's discuss the *how*. The manner in which you communicate is critical. People are listening to your tone of voice, watching your body language, and absorbing your energy when you distribute information. They are looking for hidden messages and unwritten clues as to the truthfulness of what you're saying. This is why passion, energy, and authenticity are so important in your delivery of information—if you are sharing great news but your tone sounds like the teacher who calls roll in *Ferris Bueller's Day Off*, your team will have a difficult time believing the information.

For communication to be effective and believable, the information and your energy must be aligned. As a people leader, you are the person your team looks to for insight into the validity and quality of what's being said, so you must show true human emotion when you speak in order to elicit the response you want. The same goes with sharing bad or unpleasant news: you can disseminate facts with a serious tone while still keeping your team focused and motivated toward hope for a better future. This does not mean that you should sugarcoat what you have to say, however; an overly gushy delivery will make people think you're lying or being fake in some way. Coming across as uncaring or too matter-of-fact, on the other hand, can be interpreted as arrogance, which will make your audience tune you out.

The bottom line is, the more passionate, energetic, and authentic you are in your delivery, the more your team will connect with and trust you—and that will increase your group's overall productivity and performance.

Communication in Action

One year at Nortel, the results of a company-wide survey showed that the employee satisfaction (ESAT) with the company was steadily declining. This came as quite a surprise because the leadership at Nortel had always prided itself in the fact that ESAT scores were consistently between 70 and

75 percent, which is high for a company of 30,000-plus employees. In this specific year, they dropped to well below 60 percent—a 10 percent decline from the previous year.

When the CEO at the time looked into why we had experienced such a sharp decline in employee ratings, he discovered that it was because employees felt that they were not receiving important information in a timely manner—and sometimes not at all. They felt that they were being sheltered from the real goings on in the company, and as a result they were losing morale and the motivation to do their best on the job.

In an effort to drive the ESAT back to where it had been, our CEO decided to make communication one of the company's top ten priorities for the year. He held a global employee conference call in which he shared the ESAT results and his executive team's plans for tackling the communication issue; outlined the series of brainstorming sessions his leadership team had held on how they could improve communication throughout the company; and explained to us that because this was so important to him, he was personally committing to chairing quarterly all-employee meetings/conference calls to report on company performance and other important updates as well as sending frequent e-mails about the progress of our company goals and objectives, including major customer revenue deals.

As the year progressed, our CEO did a fantastic job of delivering on all the actions he'd outlined. Each quarter, he held conference calls to share news about the company's performance and offer updates on the company's financial status. Unfortunately, though, he communicated with the employee base as if he were reporting to Wall Street. He failed to realize that many of the people on the calls were not familiar with financial jargon, and because of this, much of what he said went over people's heads and left many individuals feeling confused and—quite frankly—stupid. Worse, his delivery was so dry that no one could get a sense if what he was reporting was good or bad news. He was not connecting with his audience at all. His intent was good, but because he did not take his audience into consideration, all his efforts made little to no headway in addressing his employees' satisfaction regarding communication.

Also as promised, our CEO sent frequent e-mail updates that provided high-level information about how we as a company were stacking up against the major goals for the year. Any time a customer signed a contract or placed an order for a large telecommunication system, we heard about that too. And the information was actually quite interesting and useful. However, over time it became clear that what he was reporting was only half of the picture: the good news. Most of us knew that we were missing goals and that our performance was not as rosy as our CEO was making it out to be. And the customer deals he was reporting? Those were based on contracts being signed—contracts we all knew would not be delivering actual revenue to the company until two or three years down the road. Some of the contracts actually fell through at a later date, and we never heard about it from the CEO. After getting tired of seeing only part of reality, most employees began to hit the delete button when they saw e-mail communications from the CEO in their inboxes. Once again, the CEO's well-intentioned plan fell short on effectiveness.

Our CEO, of course, was not aware of his employees' frustration with his communications. He felt very proud of himself and his leadership team for doing what they said they would do to improve communication. He was sure that his efforts would produce better results in the next employee satisfaction survey—so, when that year's results came out and he saw that Nortel's ESAT had declined another few points from the previous year, he was shocked. When he learned that communication was still the main culprit for that score, he was so disappointed that he axed his communication plan altogether and went back to the way things had been before.

Ultimately, this CEO's intent was spot-on, but his execution fell short. He recognized and acknowledged the importance of communicating—he just failed to appreciate that he needed to mold his content and delivery style to his audience. He was missing the critical piece that would have impacted satisfaction the most.

People Leadership Action Steps to Communicate, Communicate, Communicate

1. Think about how you share information with your team. With what frequency do you share? Is there information you withhold from them? If so, why?

2. Come up with some steps you can take to improve communication with your people.

3. Think of the most effective communicator you've ever witnessed. What made him or her such a good communicator? How did his or her communication impact you?

"The art of communication is the language of leadership."

—James Humes

8

Be Innovative

Motivational speaker and author Tony Robbins says, "If you do what you've always done, you will get what you've always gotten." And yet many of us prefer to operate under the model of "If it ain't broke, don't fix it." We feel content with adhering to the status quo because just thinking about changing things is too scary. Being effective, productive, and profitable requires moving the yardstick forward, however. Being innovative—looking for better and new ways of doing things all the time—is your progress provider.

You don't have to be Steve Jobs to be an innovator. The ability to see things differently and do them more effectively is inside every one of us. As a people leader, it is your duty to be a role model and to encourage your team to think outside of the box. Create a comfortable and creative working environment in which the mantra is, "There is no such thing as a dumb idea." Encourage your team to embrace the fact that some of our craziest ideas turn into our greatest ones. If you want your organization to be more productive and profitable, innovation is a *must*.

Innovation requires that you:

- Question with curiosity.
- Be open to seeing through the eyes of another.
- Let go of what's old and outdated and create something new and better.

Question everything.

All change begins with asking questions. Innovation requires the innocence of a three-year-old child, who responds to every answer we give him or her with a "Why?" or "Why not?" This way of approaching the world forces us to examine and be curious about the reasons for our actions. When you take the time to question—not accusingly, but curiously—you will most likely find areas in your businesses that could benefit from an overhaul or remodel.

As you begin to question, be mindful that doing so can make others feel threatened. Reassure your team members that the questions are not personal attacks, accusations, or judgments—that they are solely for the purpose of uncovering old ideas and creating space for new ones. Help your team understand how innovation might make their jobs easier, more productive, and less stressful. Encourage them to adopt the practice of curiously questioning everything into their own work. Make them feel a part of the process by trying out a few of their ideas. If they work, great; if they don't, ask what caused them not to work. Bring the questioning child into your team's work habits, and watch the innovation start to ignite.

See it from someone else's point of view.

Curiously questioning the how and why of your present situation gives you a one-dimensional insight into your organization; innovation requires more of a multidimensional flair. Expand your perspective by looking at your current practices through the eyes of another person or organization. For instance, if you have a policy that impacts a customer, put yourself in the customer's shoes and ask things like "How does this rule or policy make me feel?" "Does this make my life easier or does it cause me frustration and pain?" "Do I enjoy doing business with this company, or do I want to run to their competitor?"

Remember, too, that there are other departments in your company—like sales, finance, and operations, etc.—that may be impacted by your actions and behaviors. We can sometimes get so laser-focused on doing things that will make our lives easier that we inadvertently cause significant work and pain for others. Something that may seem innovative for your team, for example, may in fact cause major disruption to another team within your organization. True innovation requires us to realize that change must always be done for the greater good. This means that before we make a change, we should always take inventory of the individuals or groups that could be impacted by it and weigh all the pros and cons before enacting it. Effective innovation is not exclusive; to make a truly positive and significant impact, it must be all-inclusive.

Let go of the old to make room for the new.

"Sacred cows" are those business practices, beliefs, and processes that have been around forever and yet serve no useful purpose. When you curiously question and see your surroundings from many dimensions, these bovines will quickly rear their ugly heads, and you will witness just how prevalent the "If it ain't broke, don't fix it" mentality is in your organization. But true innovation requires letting go of sacred cows—no matter how difficult it is to do it.

It is stunning how quickly people will attempt to protect practices that have been in existence for a long time, often with no understanding of why they are in place to begin with. Our natural tendency is to lobby for the status quo; it's comfortable, and we know exactly how it impacts our lives. People leaders, however, understand that we must teach people how to think differently if we want them to let go of the current way of doing things. This is where the fun begins. Imagine that you and your team have a fresh canvas on which to paint a new way of operating. Or maybe picture yourself as a fish that has just been let out of a small aquarium and released into the expansive ocean. There are loads of new possibilities and opportunities.

There are four steps to creating your new process or policy: 1) Outline what is currently working well; 2) Identify any sacred cows that need replacing; 3) Acknowledge the needs and wants of your customers, both internally and externally; and 4) Brainstorm new ways of doing things. Once you are finished designing the new process, take it for a test drive. Implement it with caution, so that your team and anyone else who will be impacted by the changes going into effect will have time to get used to them and to tweak the process as necessary.

People leaders who expect and encourage innovation will create highly productive and performance-driven teams.

Innovation in Action

Over the course of my career, I led several process excellence teams. These teams were responsible for finding new and better ways of doing things in order to improve employee productivity and, ultimately, save the company money. We supported the Enterprise division of Nortel, which sold telecommunication systems to businesses.

One of the operational areas our senior leaders asked us to focus on one year was the performance of our customer ordering process. They were not pleased with the results of our automated systems and processes. They had discovered through performance metrics that although we received 85 percent of our customer orders electronically, through the use of EDI (Electronic Data Interchange), a human had to complete the ordering process 60 percent of the time. This human intervention (or "touch") not only created delays in entering the order, but also generated a cost associated with each touch by an order manager. The executives called this project Touchless Ordering and asked me to champion it on the company's behalf.

I chose two of my team members, Tim and Carly, to be the coleaders of this program, and I told them it was their responsibility to innovate and improve the ordering process to minimize human intervention and delays. As they began to look into the problem, one of the first things that piqued their curiosity was the question of what was causing the orders to be stopped in the first place. Tim and Carly knew our order management system was designed to perform a series of automatic checks against the data the customer sent us in their electronic purchase order. Based on this system automation, the only orders that should be stopping were those that had problems, like incorrect pricing, or product part numbers or dates.

In an effort to isolate the issue, Tim and Carly created reports that indicated the reason for the stopped orders. They discovered that for some reason there was a system hold at the customer level for a large majority of these orders. This system hold prevented automatic checks from kicking in, which meant that a human had to look at the order before it could be processed. Nothing in the system gave Tim and Carly insight into why those customers were being placed on hold, so they began to interview the order management team (the people responsible for entering the customer orders) in the hopes that they could provide some answers.

Tim and Carly soon discovered that it was a standard practice for orders from new customers to be stopped and manually checked for accuracy by an order manager, so a system hold was entered at the customer level by the IT team every time a new customer placed an order. This was only supposed to happen for the first thirty days after a new customer entered the system, and it was designed so that both the customer and the order manager would feel confident that the EDI process was functioning with no bugs. Tim and Carly agreed that this practice made sense at first, but when they singled out a particular customer and asked the order manager how long they had been sending their orders through EDI, she responded, "Oh, over a year." That meant that for over a year, every single order from that customer was being stopped for manual review and the automatic checks were being bypassed.

Tim and Carly delved a little further and asked how many orders were typically found to have a problem—and as it turned out, it was only one or two a day out of a hundred. They repeated what they'd heard back to the order manager: "You receive one hundred orders a day and only two of them require any action on your part. Is this correct?"

"Yes," the rep said. "It seems like a waste of time to me, but that is the way it has been for over a year, so I thought it was the way it was supposed to be."

There it was: Tim and Carly had uncovered a sacred cow. Placing the customer on manual hold was supposed to be a temporary solution for new EDI customers, but somewhere along the line the order management team had begun to think of it as the standard process for all orders, and it became a permanent practice. Armed with this information, Tim and Carly immediately changed the system to remove the manual hold for any customer that had been processing EDI orders for over sixty day—and the number of orders being stopped dropped from 60 percent to 45 percent. That's a 15 percent improvement with just one change!

Tim and Carly didn't stop with just one innovative solution; after they lifted the manual hold, they reviewed the remaining 45 percent of the orders being stopped. Their report had shown that those remaining orders were failing the automatic system checks because of incomplete or incorrect information (wrong dates, wrong product part numbers, or wrong prices), but it was unclear why so many customers were sending incorrect information. Again, they became curious and asked the order managers for feedback. "The customer is just sending it wrong," the order manager said—but Tim and Carly felt that the root of the problem couldn't solely be placed on the customer. Someone in Nortel had to be providing the customer with the information they were using to place their order; the process, therefore, must be broken at another internal source point.

As they discussed their thoughts with various order managers, Tim and Carly asked them to put themselves in their customers' shoes. They asked questions like "Why do you think the customer might be putting the wrong information in their order?" and "Who gives them the data?" In these discussions, it became apparent that the communication process between Nortel and the customer was inefficient. For over ten years, Nortel had been sending manual and electronic part and price information to their customers sixty days prior to a change being introduced. The files included information on new and expiring products, as well as price changes. When the customer received the data, they automatically updated their systems. Up until this project, everyone assumed the advance notice about part and price information changes was effective because customers liked it and no problems had been reported. But Tim and Carly's fact-finding mission revealed that because the part and pricing files on new products didn't clearly indicate that those products were not yet available, customers assumed the product was orderable as soon as they received the file announcing the product. In other words, a number of customers were ordering products before they were available.

In order to resolve this issue, Tim and Carly partnered and brainstormed with the product and pricing team. Together, they decided that by simply including information about availability dates in the files sent to customers, they could eliminate confusion. This simple innovation and new way of doing things enabled an additional decrease in the order error issues.

Ultimately, by questioning the status quo, Tim and Carly improved Nortel's automated ordering process by over 23 percent; the number of orders being "touched" by an order manager decreased from 60 percent to 37 percent. All told, these improvements delivered well over $100,000 per year in cost savings to the company.

People Leadership Action Steps to Being Innovative

1. Think about how you can apply innovation in your organization. Are there any practices in your company that need a boost or a change? Have you really questioned why you are still doing them the way you do them?

2. Encourage your team to be innovative. How can you support them to be more creative?

3. Think of a time when you witnessed innovation in action. What results did it deliver to your company?

"Innovation distinguishes between a leader and a follower."

—Steve Jobs

9
Listen

"The most basic of all human needs is the need to understand and be understood," listening expert Ralph Nichols once said. "The best way to understand people is to listen to them." Since we are leading people, we need to provide a listening environment for our teams.

People leaders can create a listening environment in the workplace by:
- Giving focused attention.
- Being compassionate and discreet.
- Being a sounding board.

Give focused attention.
According to the International Listening Association, most of us spend about 75 percent of the time that we should be listening being distracted, preoccupied, or forgetful. In order to be good listeners, we must drop the multitasking and focus on the person talking. This includes turning off all distractions—laptops, tablets, cell phones—and refraining from interrupting or completing others' sentences.

Listening to others' words and thoughts rather than our own is something that takes practice, and it's an area where I am constantly working to improve. My brain wants to be two steps ahead of what people are telling me because I so want to be helpful—but this is not a good practice, even though my intentions are pure. In order to understand someone, we have to listen to what he or she is saying, and this requires focusing our attention exclusively on the other.

Be compassionate and discreet.

Listening requires compassion and discretion. There may be times when your team members need to share important information about their personal lives with you. Mixing the profession with the personal is often frowned upon in the business world—but your team needs to know you care about their whole being, not just the body that shows up for work. When it comes to listening, your role as people leader is to allow a space for your team members to bring personal concerns to you, especially if they feel it may have an impact on their work. Assure them that they can speak to you in confidence, and that doing so will not leave them open to retribution.

Allowing someone to open up to you in confidence can be very uncomfortable for you personally and may sometimes require action on your part. If a team member tells you he had a disagreement with one of his children that morning and he is frazzled, you may simply choose to listen. If she is disclosing details about abuse or other serious issues, on the other hand, you will need to empathetically suggest that she contact a professional. In some organizations, this can be done by referring an employee to human resources or to an employee assistance program; in smaller businesses, you may simply have to recommend that the employee search for outside help on his or her own. Ultimately, only you know your comfort level in listening to the details of people's personal lives.

Many leaders don't encourage their employees to disclose anything other than business concerns, and I think that's a mistake: letting each of your employees know that you are interested in him or her as a whole person establishes a strong relationship of trust between the two of you. Honoring that trust means never sharing the details your team members disclose to you with anyone else, unless your team member is a threat or a danger to him or herself. Remember, they are sharing with you *in confidence*—so the details should be kept between you and that person only.

Be a sounding board.

Being a sounding board for your team means that you listen to individuals' ideas or frustrations and reflect back to them what you hear them saying. You are not offering your own opinions or advice unless they ask you for them, nor are you shutting them down by making them feel small or unimportant when they share.

Genuinely listening to your team members' input about a problem or a solution enables them to: 1) Vent their frustrations before infecting the greater team with their negativity and doubt; 2) Ask questions without the fear of looking stupid in front of their peers; 3) Get your thoughts and guidance on a situation before they make a naive or unintended error in judgment with a larger audience; and 4) Feel heard, which gives them a sense of purpose in the organization.

As a people leader, I always encouraged my team to come to me any time they wanted to vent or were unclear about what direction to take. When an employee came into my office or called me to "talk," I made him or her feel as welcome as possible. Sometimes I'd ask, "Are you here for advice or do you just need me to listen?" Many times all that person needed was to know that I was there to listen—to be his or her sounding board. In these cases, the employee got the chance to vent, and he or she left our conversation feeling better (and therefore able to get back to productive work). If the employee was there for guidance and input, I let him or her talk first, and then we discussed solutions for whatever issue he or she was facing together.

As leaders, we are busy with our own goals and agendas, so listening is often the last thing we want to do. (It's much easier to avoid questions and tell someone what to do, after all.) Over the years, however, I learned that my organization performed far better when my team members knew they could come to me and be heard; in other words, I didn't have time *not* to listen.

Listening in Action

As pressure to improve profitability heightened, Nortel searched for new ways to cut manufacturing and distribution expenses. One of the most popular methods of cutting costs was by outsourcing operational activities to a third-party company. When Nortel entered into agreements to do business with these companies, my project team was asked to champion the program for the customer operations team to ensure that the change was implemented with minimal to no impact to our customers.

One project I worked on involved moving the distribution of a series of telephone system products and software from the United States to Canada. As was customary, I chose a person from my team to be the day-to-day lead for this particular project—in this case Olivia, one of my Canadian team members. I knew she had the expertise and skill set to get the job done.

Additionally, I knew this project would be a challenge for her and would be great for her career development.

When I told Olivia she'd be heading the project, her response was, "Are you on crack?"

"What are you talking about?" I said. Then I listened for her response. She had framed her question as a joke, but I knew she was scared. This was one of the biggest projects she'd been asked to work on since her return from maternity leave.

"I don't remember all the processes and details," she said. "I'm still trying to catch up from being out for the last year."

Olivia continued to dump out a large list of doubts and concerns for another five minutes. When she finally took a breath, I said, "I understand all of the concerns you've shared. Are there any others? Do you have any further questions about your responsibility?" I wanted to make sure I gave her the opportunity to voice all of her doubts and fears before we got too far into the project.

"No," Olivia said. "I know I can do it. I just needed to vent."

We closed the call, and I encouraged her to call me if she needed any help.

In the weeks that followed, as Olivia began her work on the project, she called me a handful of other times. In the beginning, in fact, she called me almost every day. After our initial exchange of "Hello, how are you?" I'd say, "Before we get started, what do you need from me? Do you need help or just a space to vent?" This helped me understand if I just needed to listen or if she was expecting my input. In those times when she wanted to vent, I allowed her to say anything she wanted. I listened intently and worked hard to hold in my thoughts, ideas, and impressions. As she voiced her concerns, I responded with an "I see" or an "Uh-huh"—some signal to let her know I was listening and focused on her, not on another task at hand. If she needed my thoughts or guidance, Olivia asked for my help directly, and I gave her my input and ideas about how to handle a situation or issue in her project. At the end of each of our calls, I checked in with Olivia to ensure that she had gotten what she had needed before hanging up.

Although these discussions took time out of my already busy day, they were invaluable for both Olivia and me. For her, she knew that she could come to me for any reason and I would listen to what she needed. She often told me how grateful she was that I listened to her because it prevented her from lashing out in frustration at her peers and causing unnecessary difficulties and misunderstandings with her coworkers. She also shared that having me as a sounding board to bounce ideas off of was helping her learn different ways to manage the project and to solve problems. For me, our discussions served as a way for me to keep my finger on the pulse of the project. I learned a lot about the dynamics of the project team, the issues they were facing, and the progress they were making by listening to Olivia's comments. Taking the time to listen gave me peace of mind because it showed me that the project was on the right track.

These types of listening sessions continued throughout the project. The result? Olivia successfully completed the project on track and with minimal impact to our customers.

People Leadership Action Steps to Listening

1. On a scale of 1 to 10, rate what kind of listening environment do you foster in your team. Would your team agree with your rating?

2. Think about how you can be a better listener for your team.

3. Think of the best listener you know. What does he or she do? How does he or she make you feel?

"No man ever listened himself out of a job."

—Calvin Coolidge

10

Collaborate

People leadership is not a dictatorship. It is not about one individual controlling the situation or making all the decisions. People leadership requires collaboration. That means working with a group of two or more individuals to reach a common goal for the good of the many, not for the good of one person. People leaders understand that they are far more powerful and productive when they enroll others in their visions and goals.

Collaborating effectively requires:

- A desire to interact with others.
- Having a goal in mind.
- Gaining insight from every member of the team.
- Selecting and supporting the best choice for all parties.

Want to work with people.

Any collaboration begins with a genuine desire to interact with others. While this may sound obvious, it is often overlooked. We have to *want* to do what we're doing in order for any action we take to have longstanding and productive results. As a people leader, therefore, you must have a true desire to work with others.

Working with others requires reaching out for help and input. But here's the rub: you have to genuinely want that input; you can't just engage others for appearances' sake. Time and time again, I have seen leaders pretend they are interested in ideas from their team after already having made up their minds to go in a certain direction. What happens in these situations is that these leaders quickly reject every thought or solution that is presented because they never had any real intent to listen—and their team members, in turn, lose their respect for and trust in them.

There may be some situations in which you must make decisions without collaborating with your team. If that's the case, simply make the decision, communicate it with your team, and act on it. If you are a leader who's willing to genuinely engage with others, though, you should take every opportunity to collaborate with your team. Ask yourself a few simple questions: "Am I open to others' feedback?" "Am I willing to change my mind if someone else has a better solution?" "Am I willing to set aside my agenda to hear from others on my team?" If the answer to any of these is questions is *yes*, then involve your team in your decision-making process as often as possible, and take advantage of the benefits you will reap through that collaboration.

Identify your goal.

Having a goal in mind is another key to effective collaboration. Before you ask for input, be prepared to share a description of the outcome you would like to achieve. Giving your team a so-called blank canvas from which to start a brainstorming session may sound good in theory, but in reality, such lack of direction makes most individuals feel uncomfortable. It is much easier and more effective to provide a framework of what the end picture should look like—as long as you take care to provide only the "what" and not the "how." When you give specific instructions on how a goal should be accomplished, you inadvertently limit your collaborators' ability to contribute.

When you present a goal to your team, make sure it is specific and clearly stated. Let me give you some examples:

Ineffective goal: Improve our customer experience by decreasing their call wait time.

Effective goal: Decrease our customers' call wait time from ten minutes to five minutes.

Ineffective goal: Let's increase our sales!

Effective goal: Increase each customer order by $100.

In both of these "effective goal" examples, only the specific desired outcome is identified. No reference is made to how the goal is to be achieved—and that means the "how" can come from the collective ideas of the team.

Clearly identifying your goals enables your team to provide tangible ideas and solutions, which results not only in more effective collaboration but also in more desirable results.

Get your team members' insight.

With a clear outcome in mind, you are equipped to solicit insight from all of your team members. People leaders are more effective when they receive individual viewpoints from all of the collaborators involved, not just the stars on the team. In order to do this, it is important to recognize that there are different personality types on every team.

Before beginning any collaborative activity, it may be useful to have your team take a personality inventory. One of the most extensive and well-known tools is the Myers-Briggs Type Indicator. This tool measures four areas in an individual's personality: 1) Favorite World. This attribute determines where one is most comfortable interacting. Is the person more comfortable focusing on the external or internal world? The result is either E for extrovert or I for introvert. 2) Information. This trait describes how a person processes basic information. Do they take things at face value or add their meaning to it? The result is either S for sensing or I for Intuition. 3) Decisions. This quality defines how a person makes decisions. Do they look at logic or people and special circumstances when making decisions? The result is either T for thinking or F for feeling. And finally, 4) Structure. This characteristic reveals whether an individual prefers a more structured environment, in which things are decided for them, or one that's more adaptable and open to new ways of doing things. The results for this category is J for judging or P for perceiving.

When an individual takes the Myers-Briggs test, they will end up with a label that contains one letter from each of the four categories. So, for example, they might end up with "IITP," which means they are introverted, intuitive, thinking, and perceiving. This type of person may appear to be very quiet and disinterested during a meeting, but they probably have some amazing input and ideas because they are so adept at thinking and are open to new ways of doing things.

It is great fun—and well worth the effort—to have your team members take these inventories to discover information about themselves and their peers. Collaboration is easier and more effective when your team has this knowledge in hand because it teaches everyone to understand and appreciate the differences in each of their colleagues.

In every brainstorming session I've ever led, there has always been at least one person who's dominated the conversation: the so-called extrovert. That individual is usually seen as the expert, and his or her peers are often comfortable letting him or her do all the talking. Because of this, it can be tempting to think that the input of the extroverts is an accurate representation of the entire team's thoughts—but that is never the case. It's imperative, therefore, to get *everyone* to share his or her ideas. Remember, because their tendency is to "sit back and watch," it's the quiet ones who often see important details that the louder voices on your team might have overlooked. Get them to speak up; ask them questions to get them to talk, or ask them to write down their thoughts. As a people leader, it is your responsibility to include all the personalities on your team and to keep one personality type from dominating every meeting.

People leaders understand that different personalities offer different and valuable input, and they encourage even the perceived introverts on their teams to engage in collaboration. In order for collaboration to be effective, every member of your team must feel he or she is a part of it.

Choose the best option for the greater good.

In collaboration, creating a final solution requires choosing the best option to meet your desired outcome. As your team shares their ideas and thoughts, the answer will present itself. One of the most effective ways to make this happen is to write all the suggestions down and post them for the group to see. In person, use a whiteboard or Post-it notes; if you are on the phone or are video conferencing, you can share via e-mail or screen sharing. As your team sees and reviews the various scenarios, encourage them to look for commonalities. Ask them to pick the top three to five ideas they have come up with, then outline and weigh the pros and cons of each of them and assess each idea's potential success rate. Finally, ask your team to choose their final solution.

If your team cannot come to an agreement about which idea to implement, as the leader, you may need to make the final decision— but you can do so knowing that you are choosing from your group's top three to five choices, which means they'll be more likely to support your selection than they would be if you had simply dictated it to them without asking for their input.

Collaboration in Action

After my first year at Nortel, Gary, the director of operations, gave me the job of choosing a new supply chain system to replace our myriad of homemade technology solutions. At the time, there were separate systems for each function: order management, finance, planning, and warehouse operations. We had disconnected systems because our division was a startup, and when we formed, we'd just leveraged the technology that was already in place in the company because it was convenient and cost nothing to use. The spaghetti junction of systems the team members were using was extremely cumbersome, however: because there were separate systems for each function, we had to enter the same customer and order information four times in order to have it recorded everywhere.

The process that was required went something like this:

Step 1: An order manager entered the initial customer order for the telephone system in the order entry system.

Step 2: A warehouse clerk received a paper copy of the list of products the customer needed and entered it into the warehouse system so the physical product could be picked and shipped.

Step 3: Finance received a report of all the orders entered and all the orders shipped, and they manually keyed the transactions into their system so the revenue and cost information could be reported.

Step 4: The inventory planning team received reports of inventory from the warehouse and reports about orders shipped and entered the information into an Excel spreadsheet to plan the inventory that needed to be purchased.

Gary was appalled by how much manual keying and rekeying of the same information was necessary with this system, and rightly so— what a waste of valuable time and resources. More important, he knew that as the sales and order volumes in the division grew, our team would need more flexible, agile processes and systems.

Gary tasked me with designing a process and system that would enable our division to process our customer orders from receipt to delivery to revenue recognition. This was the first major project of my career, and since Gary had not assigned me a team of people with which to do this, I thought—naively—that it was all on my shoulders to get results for the business. So I just jumped right in and began researching our options.

This was before the days of the Internet, so in order to get the information I needed, I had to make phone calls to technology vendors around the country asking them about the features and benefits of their computer software programs. Each time I talked with these vendors, they asked me for a requirements document that clearly outlined my organization's needs and desired outcomes. I had no such document. I was not even sure I knew what kind of automated solution we needed. It quickly became apparent to me that even though I had just started, I was already in *way* over my head!

I knew I had to ask some coworkers for their input, so I interviewed the decision-makers in the departments the system needed to support: order management, finance, warehouse operations, and planning. Each leader provided thoughts based on his or her understanding of the process, and after a few days of this, I had created our needs-and-desired-outcomes list. I was so proud of myself; I could now confidently ask the technology vendors to come in and present about how their systems could fulfill our needs.

After all the demos and several additional collaboration sessions, the leadership team and I chose the best system for our collective needs. I was feeling extremely confident about our decision. Now that the system had been chosen, however, it was time to design the process to work with it. Because neither the decision-makers nor I knew very much about the detailed processes or workflow, I held a series of sessions with the employees responsible for the existing process—in other words, those doing the actual work. After a few meetings, I had learned that our new system was going to negatively impact the order managers' workflow—in fact, the new technology was actually going to increase the time it would take them to complete a customer order. Yikes!

I had interviewed the leaders of these departments; how could the real need be so different from the leaders' perceptions of the need? I felt panicked and frustrated at the same time. I stormed into Gary's office and shared my dilemma, complaining that I had made a mistake by listening to the department heads. I had selected the new system based on the assumption that these leaders were well versed in the inner workings of their teams, but now it seemed that they were completely disconnected from their groups' day-to-day operations and therefore did not really understand their needs. They only understood the high-level requirements of their departments, not the detailed process needs. Because of this gap, our system choice was going to cause chaos—not only within our organization, but also with our customers. I was sweating bullets and feeling a bit defensive. After all, I felt I had done the best that I could by collaborating with the team leaders directly.

Gary listened to all my whining and pleading, and then he taught me an important and humbling lesson in people leadership. "Did it ever occur to you," he asked me, "that it was your responsibility as leader of the program to ask all of the stakeholders for input, not just the heads of the departments? You should have been the one to include the employees in the conversation before making your final selection. As project leader, it's your job to drive the collaboration with all interested parties."

I was speechless. Gary continued by saying, "It's fortunate you brought this to my attention early, because it's not too late for you to work with the vendor to make needed modifications and customizations to the system. Just make sure you include the employees' requirements to create the right solution this time."

With my tail between my legs and my ego a bit deflated, I followed Gary's advice and began holding follow-up sessions with each employee to make sure I understood his or her job and how we might tweak the system or the process in the future. It was an amazing lesson for me, and it was fascinating to see how different personalities can impact something as simple as order process workflow. I encountered outspoken naysayers who gave me every reason in the book as to why the new system would *never* work; I received input from other members who were open to anything new and were simply excited to be asked for their opinions; and then there were those for whom it was like pulling teeth to get them to talk—but when they finally opened up, their insight and recommendations proved invaluable.

After my interviews with employees from every department, I had a host of ideas on how to create a new and improved process and workflow. With those ideas in mind, we worked together as a team to implement the best choices to meet our goal of providing our customers with fast, efficient, and effective order processing. And when we finally implemented our new system, it was a success. We had our share of issues, of course, but when they arose, we worked through them together—and the result was a far more streamlined system.

Let my mistake be your reward. Any major project or change is going to impact people in all areas of your organization. If you want your program to be the most effective and efficient it can be, identify and collaborate with the key stakeholders.

People Leadership Action Steps to Collaborating

1. Describe your collaboration with your team. How do you solicit input from your team members?

2. Think about your process. What steps can you take to collaborate more effectively?

3. Describe a project or a team in which you achieved successful collaboration. What actions did you take to make the environment a collaborative one? How did your team react to the process?

"If everyone is moving forward together, then success takes care of itself."

—Henry Ford

11

Exude Confidence

People leadership cannot exist without personal confidence. Self-assuredness is not something we are born with, however—it is a trait we develop over time. As you develop your competence in specific areas, your personal confidence grows, and the effectiveness of our actions in any situation is directly linked to how competent we feel. In fact, confidence is the cornerstone of your organization's success. If you do not believe in or act confidently in your abilities, how can you expect your team to follow and engage with you? Your team takes their cues from your actions and how you portray yourself. Their confidence levels feed off of your confidence levels.

Exuding confidence requires:

- Recognizing insecurities.
- Taking action outside your comfort zone.
- "Faithing" it till you make it.

Recognize your own insecurities.

Having confidence requires knowing what you are not confident about—being open and willing to discover your personal fears and doubts. Here's the thing: Everyone has them. You're not alone! So be willing to ask yourself, *What stops me from believing in my abilities? Why am I unsure of myself in certain circumstances?* When you start receiving answers from within, be willing to listen and acknowledge the insight.

As you pay close attention to your actions and feelings, you will find that most of your concerns are based on a fear of something. Psychologists have found that there are three basic kinds of fear: fear of loss, fear of outcome, and fear of process. In their simplest form, each one of these fears is about the fear of change.

Fear of loss occurs when you feel you may lose something you currently have as a result of your efforts and actions. Fear of outcome is the dreaded fear of the unknown, the concern that whatever result you achieve will cause you some sort of pain. Finally, fear of process is when you fret that the journey of implementing what you want will cause some sort of pain. Each of these fears is usually coupled with worries you're probably more familiar with—fear of being wrong, disliked, or looking stupid, for example. Many of our insecurities are driven by group mentality or social culture. When an individual emits a nervous energy, we all feel it, and it is very contagious. That is why it is so important as a people leader for you to be in touch with your insecurities. Once you can see your fears for what they are, they are easier to overcome.

As I learned more about personal fears, I discovered that I had a tendency to overthink situations and often dismiss potentially positive changes. I always convinced myself that I was doing this because I had calculated that a good outcome would not be possible—but what I learned was that this was just fear of outcome. This insight into myself empowered me to see my constant dismissal of new ideas as nothing more than fear.

When I shared my new findings about myself with my team, they were shocked at first. Their silence told me that they were wondering why I would be divulging this to them. Wasn't I their "fearless" leader? Ultimately, however, by showing my vulnerability, I gave my team members space to get in touch with their own insecurities and helped them start down the path to personal confidence.

Walk through the fear.

The best way to exude confidence is to do what is not comfortable for you. Doing the same thing over and over again is playing it safe. While it may make you feel good, repeating your same old ways of doing things displays comfort instead of confidence. Your team gets their fuel from your energy. Be bold! All you have to do is take action.

Have you ever heard the song "Do It Anyway" by Martina McBride? The point of the song is that no matter how awful a situation seems, you shouldn't let it stop you from moving forward with your actions. This is a great mantra to use when the ugly face of fear presents itself. Instead of avoiding an activity, project, task, or discussion that you don't want to do, just take the steps to make it happen. Be careful not to overthink and over-analyze the situation. That is just fear's delay tactic—and once fear assumes control of your consciousness, you will feel it is difficult to move forward. So don't let fear stop you in your tracks. Move forward with a positive attitude and the confidence that you can do anything. It doesn't matter whether you succeed or fail; it's the action that busts your fear, not the result. Just remind yourself that no matter what happens, acting means drawing one step closer to your desired outcome. And remember to recognize and reward yourself for moving forward: your confidence grows with practice and loving care!

"Faith" it till you make it.

There are times when you will need to "faith" it until you make it. Some people call this "faking it" till you make it, but I prefer the word "faith" in place of "fake" because it is the belief in yourself that truly puts fear in its place. I love *Miracle on 34th Street*, the classic Christmas movie in which a mother and daughter have to examine their belief in Santa Claus when Kris Kringle is put on trial for lunacy after insisting that he is the "real" Santa Claus. "Faith is believing in things when common sense tells you not to," the mother tells her daughter. And this applies in business as well, as unlikely as that might seem. As a leader, you will at some point be faced with so much self-doubt that you'll have to step out of common sense and into complete faith.

If you are feeling uncomfortable in your role as leader, you must believe in your abilities—and if you're having difficulty with that, you may have to actually trick yourself into playing the part of a confident leader. There are not many times when I recommend being anything less than truthful and authentic, but this is one of them. Faking (or "faithing") it till you make it simply means that you move forward and live life as if the situation is already comfortable to you. Just make the decision as if you are already the person that you need to be. You will be amazed at how easy it can be.

Exuding Confidence in Action

In my fourth or fifth year at Nortel, my boss asked me to represent our department in an executive review meeting in Dallas, Texas. He explained to me that the meeting was to be a goal-setting and strategy session for the second half of that year, and that a mix of sales, marketing, research and development, and product management vice presidents would be there. I was excited just to be asked; I had never traveled on business before, and it was something I'd always wanted to do. We discussed the ideas and input that I should offer in the session, and by the time I left for Dallas, I felt prepared and confident to represent our team well, even though I did not have a leadership role or a fancy title.

The minute I arrived at the Dallas office, however, I started feeling a hollowness in the pit of my stomach. Every cell in my body screamed, *Danger! Danger! Danger!* as I walked through the front door. The office complex was ginormous, and its physical presence intimidated me. *You can't go to this meeting; you are just a low-level manager*, said a voice in my head. *You're not smart enough to be here. You are going to fail and look stupid in front of everyone.* Fear, that nasty creature, was rearing its ugly head. I had no idea what was going to happen when I was alone in a room with a bunch of executives, and every scenario I came up with did not look good. Still, I knew that as much as I wanted to retreat back to the hotel room and hide, I had to move forward. So I did.

I got on the elevator and pressed the button for the floor where the meeting was to be held. I felt an overwhelming desire to puke as the elevator doors opened. Then I was on the floor where all the executive offices were located. *Retreat! Retreat!* my mind and body were screaming. And yet, once again, I knew I had to keep moving forward. I walked down the hall, and with each step toward the conference room where the meeting was to be held, I felt smaller and smaller in both body and spirit. *Who am I to be here?* I thought. *I am just a lowly worker in their eyes. Why did my boss send me here? I am going to kill him when I get back. I just don't think I can do this. I am going to make a fool out of myself and of our department.* Yet still I kept walking to the conference room.

As I arrived at the conference room door, I worked to convince myself that my boss wouldn't have sent me there if he didn't know I could do it—that if he had faith in me, I needed to have faith in myself—and I regained a bit of my confidence. Then I opened the door and walked through it to find a table full of men, and I was petrified all over again. Here I was, a young, petite woman, walking into a room full of men who were probably my father's age or older. These guys were certainly more experienced in business than I was, and they were probably a lot smarter and more capable than I was, too. I wanted to say something like "Sorry, I'm in the wrong room!" and leave—but I thought of the confidence my boss had placed in me, and I found a seat at the table and joined the men.

I sat there sheepishly, not saying a word, as I waited for the meeting to start. Some eyebrows were raised, seeming to question why I was there; I think many of them thought that I was a secretary, there to take minutes in the meeting. I was too nervous—almost paralyzed—to tell them otherwise.

When the meeting began, we went around the room and introduced ourselves. I was horrified to learn that not only was I the only woman in the room, but I was the only person there below the vice president level as well. I was sitting at the table with the president of our division and his executive team! Talk about fear and insecurity taking control of every fiber of my body. I felt inadequate and completely out of my league. To prevent myself from running out the door, I had to keep telling myself, *Just stay focused. Listen to what they are saying. You are prepared for this meeting. Don't let them see you sweat. Just do your best.*

When it came time for me to share who I was and why I was there, I quickly said, "I'm Gina Folk, and I am representing the operations team, on behalf of our vice president," and I sat back down in my chair in five seconds flat.

I sat at the table for about thirty minutes listening as each of the executives brought up their ideas about goals for the remainder of the year. During this time, I hardly moved, and I didn't say a word. I was having a quiet battle inside my head: my courageous side was whispering to me to speak up, and my insecure side was yelling at me to stay quiet. However, as I listened to the executives' input, I realized that I actually had valuable input to offer. So I laid my fear aside and began sharing my opinions. At first, I responded safely with affirmations of "I agree, that seems like it could work." But the more I interjected, the more comfortable I got speaking to and with the group—and as my comfort level grew, my fear weakened. Finally, my fear dissipated to the point that I started being the person my boss knew could represent our team's interests: my opinionated self.

When I began sharing my thoughts like I was their peer, the executives looked surprised that I had actually spoken beyond just agreeing with what they had said. When my confidence increased and I kept talking, however, they started listening to my ideas and engaging in mutually beneficial dialogue. As the meeting continued, I felt comfortable and confident that my input was adding value to the discussion. At one point in particular, the group was talking about increasing sales with no regard to how our sparse operations team would handle the increased volume, and since I was there to do the right thing for our team, I was forced to speak up. I reminded the executives that while sales were awesome, if our team could not deliver the product, not only could we not collect the money, but we would also drive our customers to our competitors. To my relief, the executives agreed with my comment and acknowledged that Nortel needed to invest in our team if we were going to be able to manage the projected growth.

The more I spoke as the meeting went on, the more confident I felt—and the more I understood that if I had let my fear keep me silent, I would have felt deflated instead of energized by stepping through my insecurities. At the end of the meeting, the executives thanked me for being at the meeting and told me they were impressed with my input.

In retrospect, I realize this experience taught me three invaluable lessons about confidence that I have continued to use throughout my career: First, that those things I fear doing, unless they are life-threatening, are the things I most need to do in order to build more belief in myself. Second, that having faith in myself, and moving forward through my fears and insecurities, is the only way to build my confidence. Third, that my fear comes from self-doubt, and no one else can see my lack of confidence unless I let them—so I just have to "faith" it till I make it!

People Leadership Action Steps to Exuding Confidence

1. Rate your level of confidence in your abilities as a people leader.

2. If you don't feel 100 percent confident in your role, examine why. What's holding you back?

3. Come up with steps you can take to eliminate your lack of confidence.

4. Describe a time when you did feel confident in a role. What made you feel that way?

"He can inspire a group only if he himself is filled with confidence and hope of success."

—Floyd V. Filson

12
Motivate

Sustaining a highly productive and effective team that delivers excellent results requires consistent motivation. Motivation does not come in one highly energized "rah-rah" annual conference or monthly staff meeting—and while hiring a team of self-starters is always a good practice, even the most driven and disciplined people still need a catalyst to drive them to action. According to Sigmund Freud, people are moved to action for two reasons: to avoid pain or to seek pleasure. With his studies of positive and negative reinforcement, BJ Skinner proved that people's behavior changes more quickly when they are offered positive encouragement, rewards, and recognition than it does when they are motivated by fear and punishment. Freud and Skinner both agreed that no matter the inner strength of the individual, to sustain performance, they require some outside stimulus to push them forward.

Over my twenty-three-year career, I tried various motivation methods. The fear-oriented "You will meet this goal if you want to keep your job" method was fairly popular when I entered my first supervisory role; it was the method I had seen and heard about most often from my peers and other leaders. But I quickly discovered that scaring and forcing people into action in their jobs only creates problems. While the task may get completed, what people produce out of fear is generally of lesser quality—and worse, an individual who has been motivated through negative reinforcement is typically less motivated to perform the next time.

Acting out of fear pushes us to find the quickest way to make the fear go away, with no regard to the quality of the effort and outcome. It's like a child who's told that he must clean his room immediately or lose out on his playtime. My mother pulled this on me, and my response was to rush around the room and throw any item in plain sight into drawers or under the bed. I hustled to get the job done to avoid the pain of missing playtime with my friends, and the external result met my mom's approval—but my room was still a hot mess just under the surface. And motivating employees in the workplace through fear is no different. Their tasks will get done, but the quality of the work will be lacking and will likely cause quality issues or require reworking at some point in the future.

When my own efforts to motivate were met with poor quality results, I knew I had to do something different—so I attended various leadership seminars and read several leadership and self-help books in search of an answer. What I saw was fairly unanimous: people perform better and more consistently through positive support rather than negative motivation.

Through numerous experiments with my team, I discovered that effective motivation requires:

- Knowing a person's motivators.
- Expecting greatness.
- Being a consistent cheerleader.
- Recognizing people's efforts.

Figure out what motivates your team members.

As I discussed in Chapter 2, every one of us is different. Our diverse experiences and inherent traits define who we are and how we act in various situations over time. One of the personality traits we develop through our experiences is what I refer to as the "action trigger"—the spark that lights our fire, or the gas that gets our engines moving forward. As a people leader, finding your employees' action triggers is your and their key to excellent and sustained outcomes.

Finding your team members' action triggers requires getting to know them individually. It means that you must ask your people questions like "What values are important to you?" "What job or work activity did you have the most fun or feel the most energized in?" and "What causes you to be excited about coming to work and exceeding in your role?"

When you hold these conversations, listen actively to your employees' answers. Many companies assume people are most motivated by money, so they use things like bonuses, commissions, promotions, and pay increases to encourage better work. However, recent employee surveys have proven that while money is important, it is not the factor that most drives people to excel in their jobs. Honestly, I think money is more of an expected given in the workplace today rather than a motivator; by itself, it's not enough to incentivize outstanding results. Even with the promise of better pay for increased productivity, most people will come in and do just enough to keep their jobs.

So what is a true motivator? Well, what inspires one person to action may be very different from what motivates his or her peers. I did find common themes as I began to discover more about my team members' action triggers, however. When people *are* motivated by money, for example, there's usually a specific need or want attached to that: perhaps they have kids in private schools, or maybe they are preparing for a new baby. Others, meanwhile, may be motivated by feeling valued by the company. Others still may be inspired by consistent appreciation and recognition.

Once I understood and aligned the individuals on my team with the correct action triggers, the more their performance improved, which led to sustained success for them, the team, and the company.

Expect greatness.

One of my favorite bands, Matchbox Twenty, has an album called *More Than You Think You Are*. The phrase is motivation in its simplest form, and it's the core of a concept called the Pygmalion effect—the idea that the higher the expectations placed on someone, the more likely they are to exceed in their actions. The polar opposite of this phenomenon is called the Golem effect, where low expectations lead to lesser outcomes.

Audrey Hepburn and Rex Harrison showcase the Pygmalion effect in the classic movie *My Fair Lady*. Harrison's character, Henry Higgins, takes Hepburn's character, Eliza Doolittle—a flower girl in the poorest section of London—under his tutelage with the expectation of turning her from a common girl into a lady. Over time, Eliza transforms into the well-bred woman Higgins expected her to become, much to her surprise. This same result can happen in the workplace when leaders expect great things from their people.

One of the most frequent frustrations I hear when I work with companies and leaders is that their employees are not pulling their weight or living up to their standards. Whenever I hear this complaint, I respond with one simple question: "What are your expectations?" The most common answer is, "I just need them to get the job I'm paying them for done." And that right there is the problem: the leader's low expectations are causing his or her employees' low performance.

Psychologists have proven time and again that people perform to whatever expectations are established and encouraged. Low or unclear expectations, then, deliver poor results, and mediocre expectations deliver just-good-enough results. Setting high expectations leads to outstanding performance. There is a fine art to setting high expectations, though: like rubber bands, you can stretch people farther than they think they can go; however, you can't stretch them beyond their abilities, or they will snap.

Cheerlead consistently.

Establishing expectations does not deliver results on its own: people need your encouragement and belief that they can live up to the expectations you set. That's why people leadership requires consistent cheerleading. Just as players on sports teams need to hear "You can do it!" and "Go team!" from their cheerleaders and fans, employees need a steady boost of optimism from their leaders. You should always be present on the sidelines, encouraging your team, especially when the path to success gets a tad rocky.

Supporting your team members in this way requires frequent check-ins to discuss their progress. These check-ins can be as simple as sending an e-mail to ask how they're doing and how you can support them, or they can be scheduled times where you discuss any relevant updates or roadblocks on the phone or face-to-face. The method is not as important as the act of reaching out and being present.

Whatever means you choose to communicate by, be aware that if your employees respect you, they sincerely want your approval and are working hard to live up to the expectations you've established for them. So, if they make any progress, tell them you recognize it. If, on the other hand, the person falters for some reason, clarify what caused the delay, help them resolve the issue, and reassure them that you know they can do the job and that you trust in their abilities. Remind them how important their role is to the organization and how their efforts are valued.

Cheerleading includes reminding employees to keep their focus on the end result and achieving their goals—but when you do this, refrain from displaying any doubt in their abilities, even if you have some concerns. Once a person senses your disapproval, his or her performance will decline. People leaders who show their team members they are their biggest fans are the leaders who create winning and effective teams.

Recognize your team members' efforts.

People want to know that their actions are noticed and valued. One of the most effective motivators for many individuals is genuine appreciation and recognition that their effort is making a difference to the company and their leaders. One of the most common questions people ask themselves on their deathbeds is whether they mattered—and people in the workplace silently ask themselves this same question every day. The only way people can really know whether they matter is by hearing that they do from someone they trust and admire.

Your team will thrive when you offer consistent expressions of gratitude and appreciation for their work. A simple "Thank you, your hard work really made a difference" for a job well done can go a long way. And in today's electronic age, a hand-written note is often far more effective than an e-mail or text. People will appreciate the extra effort you've exerted to write and send them a letter. Even the techie generation gets a kick out of snail mail every now and then!

Offering praise to an individual in front of his or her coworkers and peers (as long as it is fair and warranted, of course) is another amazing form of recognition. Every one of us wants to know that we are doing a good job. Remember, people are pleasure-seeking creatures, and knowing that we've done something right makes us feel good—and you may be the only person in your team members' lives offering this kind of support, which will make your positivity all the more meaningful.

Motivation in Action

Lincoln, a twenty-two-year-old employee in our largest warehouse operation, had a reputation for being a very inconsistent employee. On his good days, he would complete one and a half times the work his coworkers completed; other days, however, he would slack off so much that he produced below the standards of his established objectives.

Lincoln's performance wasn't the only thing that was unpredictable: his attitude and behavior at work was erratic, too. Some days he would be in a great mood, willing to help anyone and take on any task that was assigned to him; other days he was like the Tasmanian Devil, chewing up spitting out anyone who crossed his path and leaving a trail of debris and incomplete work behind him. His attendance was consistently poor, especially on Mondays and Fridays.

Frustrated with his fickle performance, Lincoln's supervisor, Manny, came to me for guidance. Manny was at his wit's end and was poised and ready to fire Lincoln. He didn't have enough time to work with him individually, he said, and Lincoln's volatile behavior was creating motivational and teamwork challenges with the rest of his people. A "slacker" mentality was working its way through the workforce because other individuals were following Lincoln's example.

In my discussion with Manny, I asked him why Lincoln was still employed, and he immediately began listing Lincoln's exceptional qualities. I discovered that when Lincoln was in the zone, he was the most proficient shipping employee in the warehouse: he could process three times more shipments than his peers could in a day. He was also cross-trained in almost every role in the warehouse, including picking, packing, and receiving activities, because when he finished his work he got bored and went in search of activities to fill his time.

As Manny rattled off a list of Lincoln's phenomenal accomplishments, it was clear that this young man had the *capacity* to perform, but he was lacking the *desire* to do it. I wanted to perform my own assessment, so I asked Manny if I could speak with Lincoln directly about our concerns. He gladly accepted my offer; he had tried everything he could think of to get Lincoln on track, and he was ready to give up. So I invited Lincoln into my office to have a discussion.

As soon as he walked through my door and sat down, Lincoln—looking both angry and a little embarrassed—asked, "Are you firing me?"

"No, should I?" I responded.

"Nah," he said, and he swallowed a slight laugh.

Our discussion continued with questions about what was going on with his performance, behavior, and attendance. He openly shared with me that the main reason he had good and bad days was that he did not believe that what he was doing made a difference—and he said that Manny was never satisfied. If Lincoln performed great, he wanted him to produce more. If he slacked off, he got a lecture about how he should do better. When he took the personal initiative to learn various roles from his peers, Manny did not recognize him for his desire to learn more, which was frustrating for him. "Why does it matter whether I show up for work or work extra hard?" Lincoln asked. "Nothing I do is appreciated anyway."

Lincoln was placing the blame on Manny, but what I realized during this conversation was that I was at fault for the situation before me. Manny and my other supervisors were just following my lead; they weren't motivating their teams effectively because I wasn't motivating them effectively. "Get the job done or we will find someone who will" was how I had been running things. I was too focused on achieving results for the good of the company—on making my mark—to worry about offering my team members encouragement or doling out recognition for their efforts.

With that epiphany in mind, I humbly admitted to Lincoln that Manny's lack of motivating others was my responsibility. I asked him if he would agree to assist me in remedying the situation, and I could tell his energy and his attitude were already shifting—he was getting excited. "I'd be happy to help you in any way I can," he said. So I asked for his recommendations on motivating him to be a consistent employee. "Well, you can start by giving me stretch goals; they make me want to work," he said. "I don't want to be bored—I like a good challenge. Oh, and I just need to know I matter. I don't really have too many people in my life that appreciate what I do no matter how hard I try. I am not asking for much, just a thank-you every now and then. Or maybe lunch for the whole team when we all do a great job."

In that brief conversation, Lincoln taught me more about the power of effective motivation than all of the books I'd read and seminars I'd attended on leadership. And as my managers and I began to implement his suggestions, Lincoln's performance excelled! He exceeded all the objectives he was assigned, he came in each and every day with a positive attitude, and showing up on Mondays and Fridays stopped being an issue. Within a year, Lincoln had been promoted to team leader and shift supervisor.

A few years later, Lincoln left Nortel and went on to a leadership role at another company. I was thrilled to see him again when he stopped by the company's outsourced warehouse operations, where I happened to be visiting the same day. He came over, gave me a great big hug, and said, "Gina,

I want to tell you thank you for believing in me and encouraging me to exceed your expectations. Thank you for letting me know that I mattered. Your leadership meant more to me than I can express. Now I try to do the same things for the people that I manage."

For me, that was proof enough that effective motivation works and is extremely impactful!

People Leadership Action Steps to Motivate

1. List the motivators for each of your team members. Are your current methods of motivation aligned to meet their action triggers?

2. Are you expecting greatness from your team? If so, describe how. If not, ask yourself how you can change your behavior and attitude to expect great things from them.

3. How are you encouraging your team? How frequently are you doing it? Assess whether you can improve in this area.

4. Does your team know they make a difference to you and the company? Think about how you can better facilitate their knowing.

5. Think of a leader that was a phenomenal motivator for you. What did he or she do? How did his or her motivation impact your performance?

"Motivation is the art of getting people to do what you want them to do because they want to do it."

—Dwight Eisenhower

13
Guidance, Not Control

L eaders that feel compelled to make every decision and dictate every action their employees make are control freaks—or, to use a more professional word, micromanagers. In each of the numerous surveys conducted about what people hate most about their bosses, micromanaging always makes the top ten list of dislikes—and yet countless leaders engage in this behavior. Good people leaders know not to do this.

People have no desire to be controlled, but they do look to their commanders-in-chief for guidance. Your employees need someone to provide a structure and framework for them to operate within. Just like a ship needs a captain to keep it on course, employees need a leader to establish their route and steer them in the right direction. Leading through guidance instead of control means:

- Setting a direction and creating boundaries.
- Staying out of the details.
- Supporting instead of dominating.

Set a direction and create boundaries.
Strong buildings require good architectural blueprints to outline the overall plan for the structure and to define the framework that will make the building functional, and productive organizations have similar requirements. People are more purposeful and effective when they know where they are headed and understand the boundaries within which they can operate. I am

not referring to setting visions, rules, and policies that tightly dictate how a person must operate to achieve success—that's control disguised as guidance. What is truly helpful is creating a direction and crafting boundaries that offer enough leeway for people to contribute their own creative ideas and use their personal talents to achieve an outcome.

Regardless of the size of your organization, company, or project, three elements—mission, vision, and workplace values—serve as the foundation of your company's structure. The most effective missions I have seen are those that are simple and yet express the true essence of the company. For instance, Southwest Airlines' mission statement is, "Dedication to the highest quality of customer service delivered with a sense of warmth, friendliness, individual pride, and company spirit." I love this statement because it is broad enough to allow people to use their strengths and personalities to achieve the goal set forth and yet specific enough to let team members know how their efforts contribute to the company's success. When I travel, I always try to fly Southwest—not only because of the low fares but also because I know that I am going to be treated with warmth and a personal touch. Sometimes their flight attendants are simply smiling, helpful, and gracious; on other occasions they get to display their comedic or acting talents during the normally boring announcements that happen on every flight. I've been on many flights where the pilot has been there to greet me as I arrived and thank me profoundly for being part of their family. As you can see, Southwest is a stellar example of a company that has set a clear direction that allows individual expression.

Your company's direction works best when it is coupled with an operating framework that establishes boundaries within which your team can work. This includes setting individual goals for each team member that clearly define the outcome you want him or her to achieve in his or her role. A strong framework also includes parameters within which an individual can make decisions that are appropriate for his or her level of responsibility. I frequently see policies, procedures, and processes at the companies I work with that are so tight, with such strict checks and balances, that people's ability to excel in their performance is stifled. I am not suggesting that checks and balances are not important; I am recommending, however, that the boundaries you set offer enough room for team members to feel they have autonomy to do what they believe is best in a given situation. Clear direction and boundaries provide your employees with the blueprint they need to produce effective results.

Stay out of the detail.

Once you have established direction and boundaries for your employees, there is no reason for you, the leader, to be involved in the details. After all, you probably don't know as much about the day-to-day operations as your team members do—and even if you do have some expertise in a particular area or about a specific objective, your role is to lead people, not to tell them how to do it or to complete it yourself. You may feel you are helping your employees by lending an extra hand, especially if your company has downsized or restructured recently, but you're probably doing more harm than good when you insert yourself into your employees' work.

In the event that your team asks for help or you see a need for assistance, ask them how you can best support them. In the times when I had requests for help from my team and I asked them this question, I usually found that they actually wanted help from other coworkers or a change in priorities. Very rarely did they want my hands in their detailed work.

If, on the odd occasion, one of your employees asks you to pitch in, ask them to properly train you on how to do the work before jumping in. You don't want to make mistakes or leave work undone that will require more effort from your team after the fact. Unless you know exactly what and how the job needs to be done, it is best to simply set the course and leave the details to your team.

Support; don't dominate.

People leaders do not dominate their team's actions; they support and trust in their team members' individual abilities. Because many leaders are so driven to perform, they tend to be outspoken and to want to provide innovative ideas and make quick decisions in order to get the job done. Although it may be second nature and unintended, this behavior is simply another form of control. Guiding your team means letting them have the spotlight—providing them with opportunities and encouraging them to be the recognized experts and leaders in their roles.

Some employees are naturally more confident in voicing their ideas and displaying their talents openly, even when you may be dominating the situation. These individuals require little to no support from you because they are self-assured. Others on your team will look for your guidance to show them how to be bold and express themselves. In these cases, your mentoring can start with simple actions. For instance, when you are in meetings, wait and give your team space to do the talking before speaking yourself. Ask your employees to share their knowledge and expertise. If you sense hesitation, encourage them to engage by asking leading questions like "I am thinking of this solution; can you think of a reason or two that it won't work, or do you have any other better ideas?" When they start sharing their thoughts, acknowledge them for speaking up and continue allowing them to share their ideas.

This same method applies to the implementation of your team members' individual goals or work activities. Support their progress toward successfully delivering on their goals instead of dictating to them how to get the activity done. People leaders are the support mechanism for their team members, not the dominating force behind them.

No matter how tempting it may be to control your employees and their actions, remember: guiding them is always much more effective.

Guidance, Not Control in Action

Randolph, our director of customer service, was feeling overwhelmed by the sense of panic and chaos that was pervading his department. A key manager who supported one of the most difficult and demanding customers in the company left unexpectedly. Randolph did not have the time to deal with the customer demands on a daily basis, so he needed to find a replacement, and fast! Due to recent budget constraints and a hiring freeze, however, he could not hire a new person for the position; he had to fill it with an existing resource on his team.

Frantic to find someone, Randolph conducted a quick review of his current leadership team to see who had the skill set and bandwidth to serve as interim leader for this customer service group. Based on her knowledge of the customer base and key processes, he felt that Caroline was best suited to immediately fill the gap, and he asked her to step up.

When Randolph offered her the manager position, Caroline accepted, but reluctantly: she knew she was walking into a bit of a hornet's nest. She had firsthand knowledge from the employees and customers that the previous manager had offered little to no guidance and support to the team, which meant that the employees were clueless as to how to service their customers effectively. They did not understand the expectations for their roles, and they had no boundaries within which to make informed decisions to meet the company's and customers' needs. Furthermore, their team had been hit hard with recent staff cuts, and those left behind were struggling to keep up with their work. Caroline had heard horror stories from the customers who had personally complained to Randolph about the inefficiency and lack of professionalism of the team. Before she even started the role, she was feeling stressed out.

After quickly assessing her team's needs and their state of chaos, Caroline felt that the best way to support them was to become an additional workhorse on the team. After all, she knew the customers and understood the processes, and her skills with the customer ordering system were good enough to get the job done. So without asking anyone, Caroline began entering orders, answering customer phone calls, and managing customer escalations. Her entire day was consumed with picking up the perceived slack her team was leaving. However, the more Caroline engaged in the day-to-day activities, the less her team made decisions and handled the details and the more they inundated her with problems. As time went on, her to-do list grew longer and longer, and her team contributed less and less. In her effort to take control, Caroline had created an even bigger mess than she'd started with.

Caroline and I had worked together throughout the years, and we often served as each other's counsel when we needed some advice, so when things started to get really bad, she came to me. As she outlined the details of what had occurred over the previous several weeks, I quickly saw that her desire to help had actually morphed into her seizing total control, which had made her team become even less driven to perform.

"It sounds to me like you've become the doer instead of the leader," I told her.

For the next few seconds, you could have heard a pin drop on the other end of the phone. "Are you still there?" I asked.

"Yes, I just got a sick feeling in my stomach when you said that," Caroline said. "You are absolutely right. I am kicking myself right now. I just wanted to help, and instead I've made things worse!"

I reinforced to Caroline that I recognized she was trying to do the right thing, and I told her not to beat herself up too badly. I suggested she meet with her team to set a new direction and define boundaries that would allow them to restructure and re-engage in their day-to-day activities, and I reminded her that once the structure was established, her role as leader was to offer guidance and support, not to control her team and do their work for them.

Caroline left our conversation with a new energy and desire to change things on her team. It took time—and consistent and persistent guidance—for her team to embrace her shift from controller to leader, but after a few months, she reported back to me that her team was indeed taking over the day-to-day activities they were supposed to be in charge of, which freed her up to focus more on the strategic projects that she'd put on the backburner when she started her new role. Going forward, both Caroline and her team were much happier and more effective.

People Leadership Action Steps to Guidance, Not Control

1. Think about how your team would describe your approach to leadership. Would they say you are controlling or guiding?

2. Come up with some steps you can take to guide instead of control.

3. Come up with some examples of leaders you know who model this principle. What specific actions do they take? How effective are they in their role?

"Give people enough guidance to make the decisions you want them to make. Don't tell them what to do, but encourage them to do what is best."

—Jimmy Johnson

14
Manage the Personnel "Stuff"

My beloved grandfather, Poppy, used to say, "You know what the most important thing in life is? Stuff. Yep, it's almost as important as breathing." We laughed and rolled our eyes whenever he said it, but now I understand: the "stuff" he was talking about was not just the material things we surround ourselves with but all of the details of our daily lives—things like work schedules, family commitments, and everything else that consumes our time (but is also important to our fulfillment).

Poppy was right. The "stuff" he was referencing is very important to our personal identity and the quality of our lives. And when it comes to leading people, one of the most misunderstood and overlooked necessities is managing personnel "stuff." This is the art of coordinating your staff's time, talent, and energy to ensure they are organized enough to produce outstanding results. It includes things like orchestrating staff members' time off and ensuring employees' schedules match customer demands. And much like the "stuff" in our lives, doing it well is vital to the survival of an organization.

I have worked with organizations whose leaders felt that managing this type of minutiae was too menial and time-consuming—but what they failed to realize is that without the proper oversight of personnel "stuff," an organization will experience a slow decline or significant disruption in performance.

Managing personnel "stuff" includes:
- Overseeing vacation, absenteeism, and holiday coverage.
- Cross-training staff.
- Prioritizing employees' workload.

Know what's happening with vacations, absences, and holidays.

As a people leader, it is your responsibility to ensure your team can function to consistently achieve your organization's goals and objectives. In order to do this, you must have a firm grasp on your staff's time at work and how their presence, or lack thereof, contributes to the workflow and performance outcomes of your company. No matter your organization's size or type, creating and tracking your employees' work schedules, including breaks, vacations, time off, holidays, and others absences is essential.

The reason your team's schedules need coordination is not because you're trying to create a Big Brother environment for your employees; I am actually in favor of flexible work schedules, as long as they are designed with the needs of the company, its customers, and its employees in mind. Many studies have shown that taking time off and working flexible hours increases an individual's engagement in his or her job and leads to increased performance. The implementation and maintenance of your team's calendars, when executed well, should empower you and your team to minimize business interruption and maintain a consistent workflow.

The first step in mastering your team's schedule is asking questions. For instance, do your standard work hours take into consideration customer demands and behaviors? Have you thought about time zones and country holidays in the regions you support in creating your organization's work schedule? Do you offer breaks to your team members, and if so, are they orchestrated to ensure there is no gap in the workflow? What about vacations? Do all of your employees take off at the same time, creating a complete halt in productivity until they return?

Last, and certainly not least, is absenteeism. When a team member calls in sick or does not show up for work, do you know about it? Can you ensure his or her work gets covered? Are you tracking repeated absences with a team member? If someone is not showing up on a regular basis, that's probably a sign that he or she needs special attention and motivation to prevent future problems.

Crafting, coordinating, and monitoring your employees' working time is the lifeblood of your business. After all, if the people are there and the work is not, or the work is there and the people are not, your organization will not be in existence for long.

Cross-train for overall fitness.

A physically fit person is strong in a number of areas, not just one. The same principle applies to your team's productivity. Beyond scheduling, a piece of the personnel-stuff pie that is often overlooked is cross-training. In order for your organization to be at its "fittest"—in order to hone its agility, strength, and flexibility—your people must be cross-trained. With the increased workload and daily demands on workers due to job cutbacks, however, it can feel impossible to carve out time for training people in other areas; in fact, I've found cross-training lacking in almost every organization I've worked with. No matter the size of the task, anything can be done when it is made a priority—and this is one thing that should be made a priority.

Cross-training should be a top goal for every one of your team members. The benefits it reaps in the long term will far outweigh the inconveniences in the short term. Your people will develop and gain knowledge in other areas of your business, which will increase their value and self-worth—and as they grow, your organization will not only benefit from their increase in productivity but will also have the assurance that when people go on vacation or call in sick, other team members will be able to pick up their slack, preventing work stoppage and interruptions.

One simple and painless way to cross-train is to choose one role that is complementary to and supportive of an employee's current role, and then to carve out a section of his or her workday—even if it is only thirty minutes—to allow him or her to shadow his or her peer and learn the ins and outs of that role. It takes a lot less time than you think for a person to learn a new skill when he or she is encouraged, and cross-training enables your organization to be extremely flexible, which contributes to increased productivity.

Prioritize your employees' workload.

There is a tendency in many organizations to expect every work activity or project that is assigned to an individual to be treated as a number one priority—and yet there must be an order in which things should get done, because without order, nothing will get done.

Expecting everything to get done simultaneously is like a juggler throwing three balls into the air at the same time and expecting them to magically defy gravity and remain suspended. I actually learned this from experience: When I was a kid, I was watching my younger brother try to figure out how to juggle. As the older sister, I was convinced it was easy and I could do it too, so I threw three balls in the air at the same time—and down they all came. What I was too impatient to learn was that a juggler has an order, a flow, in which she tosses the balls in the air. Without that flow, keeping the balls moving is impossible—and proper assigning of work activities and projects is no different. Doing things in the order of their importance is critical, especially if you've had to make cutbacks and have fewer people doing more work.

Assigning work is a skill that requires you as the leader to understand every aspect of every major activity your team is responsible for: the purpose of the activity; the expected benefit to the customer or business; the impact that not completing the activity would have on your organization; and the available staff that could get it done. With this information in hand, you are better poised to provide guidance and prioritize the work that must get done versus the work that can be completed at a later date.

Prioritizing your team's workload is a win-win: it takes a burden off their shoulders, it shows them that you care about their success, and it increases your group's overall productivity.

Managing the Personnel "Stuff" in Action

I was sitting at my desk, intently focused on an important project update presentation, when my phone rang. Frustrated by the distraction, I looked up to see the name on the caller ID was "Fortson, Johnson."

"Crap," I muttered. "What's gone wrong now?"

Johnson Fortson was the new VP of operations, and he normally only called me when a problem escalated. This time was no exception; when I answered the phone, he immediately asked for my help. "I'm getting complaints from major customers that they are not receiving orders," he said, sounding a little frantic. "Can you fix this for me?"

"I'll sure try," I told him. "Let me get some details and give you an update tomorrow."

I was confident the problem he was referencing had to do with the major outsourcing project we had just completed. We'd moved our software manufacturing operation to an outside supplier in Canada, and as far as I knew, things were moving smoothly—but it sounded like that might not actually be the case. I immediately called Larry, the manager of the organization, and asked him to tell me what he thought of Johnson's concern.

When I got Larry on the phone, he informed me that to his knowledge his team was behind in the manufacturing process by at least two days. This meant that there were over one hundred orders that were past due. I prodded him for more details as to the root cause of the delay, and he said, "There are just too many orders. The staff can't keep up. The process and lack of training is causing bottlenecks in the workflow. Maybe you should come to the facility to look at it."

I called Johnson back with the information from Larry, and we agreed that I needed to fly to Canada to check it out. The very next day, I was on a plane to Calgary.

When I went to the factory to observe what was happening with the process, I was baffled. My first surprise when I arrived onsite was that not much activity was happening. There were at least twenty people in the manufacturing area who were not working on orders: they were organizing their workstations or chatting amongst themselves instead of making product. I did not see any bottlenecks in the process; what I saw was a complete lack of activity. This was a much different environment than Larry had described in our phone conversation.

I decided to reach out to the team leader, Harriet, to get her input as to what was happening. She explained to me that there was not much work at this time of day because customer orders did not start arriving until one to two hours after the shift began. I wanted to say, *Are you kidding me?* but I refrained and decided to keep observing and gathering information. I asked Harriet about the status of the backlog of customer orders that I could see stacked up on six shelves in the middle of the room; couldn't those be worked on during this period of the day, I wondered? But Harriet told me that all of those orders had problems, and the manufacturing team could not complete them until they received answers from the customer service team. When I asked her if customer service was not responding in a timely manner, she reminded me that the delay was due more to the differences in time zones and work schedules than to a lack of response from the order managers.

My next surprise came around 10:00 AM when everyone—and by everyone, I literally mean the entire staff on the shift—took a break. The manufacturing area cleared out and was completely empty for fifteen minutes. When the employees left the room, I found myself alone, listening to ringing phones and watching a pile of work orders for the team to produce roll out of the printer. Between the time the staff left on break and the time they returned, which was about fifteen minutes, a huge pile of new orders and voice messages had piled up. Upon seeing this, the employees' looks turned frustrated and deflated. "Look at all this work," I heard one person mutter. "Why does it always come when we aren't here? There's no way we can get this done. This is ridiculous!" I witnessed this same situation two more times that day: after lunch, and then following the afternoon break.

Throughout the day I continued to ask questions of Harriet. In our conversations, she expressed concerns that the employees were scheduled to work based on their ability to produce a certain number of orders every day. Each person was responsible for his or her own piece of the manufacturing process, so if just one person was out—whether for vacation or because he or she called in sick—the workflow stopped at his or her station until he or she returned to work. No one on the team was cross-trained to do anyone else's job.

As I continued to probe deeper into the workflow patterns with Harriet, I sensed she was getting a bit nervous. She was forthcoming in her responses to my questions around process and workflow, but every time I mentioned or questioned the staff work hours or breaks, she hesitated. At the end of our discussions for the day, she cautiously shared with me that she was just the team leader, and because of that, she had no authority over the personnel scheduling. When I asked her who was in charge of this important business task, she told me it was Larry. *Interesting*, I thought to myself, since Larry had told me the problem lay in the process and the order volume and hadn't mentioned anything about his team's hours, breaks, or dedicated work functions.

I still had not seen or spoken with Larry since arriving in Calgary. He was busy working with another one of his groups in the manufacturing facility. At this point I realized that his interpretation of the issue was not a representation of reality, but before I met with him, I wanted to make sure I had the full picture from all angles. So I interviewed every group involved in the order process workflow to ensure I had uncovered all perspectives and issues—I talked with members of the customer service team, the inventory management team, and the warehouse team. What I discovered was that it was clear to all parties involved (except, apparently, Larry) that the order backlog issues were caused primarily by three things: 1) The misalignment of employee work hours to the customer order demand; 2) The lack of cross-training within the manufacturing team; and 3) The time delays in getting responses on problem orders back from the customer service teams due to shift and time zone differences. None of these issues had anything to do with volume of orders or bottlenecks in the designed process flow.

When I shared my findings with Larry, he was shocked. He told me he had no idea that the employees' schedule or breaks were a concern. He admitted that his meeting schedules and other priorities had prevented him from going to investigate the situation himself. Together, we agreed that the scheduled hours and breaks of the Manufacturing team needed to align with the customer order patterns, and that customer service team schedules needed to allow a constant flow of work throughout the day. Larry also committed to working with Harriet to stagger the manufacturing team's breaks and lunch hour to enable the process to continue to operate. Lastly, we created a cross-training plan for each team member to teach him or her one other function in the workflow. This improvement allowed for backfilling specific functions in the event an employee was absent.

I updated Johnson about our progress, feeling good about the plan Larry, Harriet, and I had created. He was pleased and confident with the resolution and looked forward to seeing positive results. A few weeks after implementing the plan, order backlog decreased to an all-time low since the start of the project, and customer orders were being completed within the expected time frames.

People Leadership Action Steps to Managing Personnel "Stuff"

1. Consider your staffing plan. How well is it aligned to the needs of both your customers and your business?

2. Do you have an effective tracking tool to keep up with vacations, time off, absences, and holidays? Come up with some steps you can take to create a more effective system for you and your team.

3. How can you integrate cross-training into your team? Design a plan.

4. Do you have a prioritization system that works effectively for your team? Would they agree? If not, think about how you might rework it.

5. Describe the most successful manager you know that kept up with all the personnel "stuff" in his or her group. How did he or she do it? What impact did his or her diligence have on the team?

"A good leader is not the person who does things right, but the person who finds the right things to do."

—Anthony T. Padovano

15

Use Power Wisely

When left to my own devices, I am not disciplined enough to push myself to uncomfortable limits; so, in order to stay physically fit and healthy, I make it a priority to have a personal trainer in my life. I'm surprised at how often the things he says to me apply brilliantly not only to my workouts, but also to leadership. One day, in the midst of a very challenging, fast-paced cardio/weights circuit—at a point when I was huffing and puffing, about to puke and ready to quit—he yelled, "Faster, faster! Push harder, push, push, push. Come on, Gina! Strength plus speed equals power!" Although I wanted to reach out and smack him for driving me so hard, I couldn't refrain from telling him in the moment how applicable this definition of power was to people leadership.

Unfortunately, power is often misconstrued and misused in business, politics, and society as a means to exert brute force over another person or situation in order to get results. While using power in this way can deliver immediate results, it's rare that performance elicited by these methods is sustainable or effective in the long term. Power must be used wisely to produce the best results for the greater good.

Using power wisely requires:
- Moving from a position of strength.
- Moving forward swiftly.
- Maintaining your progress.

Move from a position of strength.

In business, your position of strength comes in two forms. First is the intention and purpose of your actions and decisions; second is the expertise you apply to them. Intention in this respect means that you have a clear picture of the direction in which you want to head. This can be in the form of a vision, goal, or simply the purpose behind any activity.

Given the fact that every book on leadership and good business talks about vision, it is surprising how seldom it is actually put into practical use. And yet creating powerful results requires having a planned outcome that has been clearly communicated to each person who will be part of creating the end result. Every intention is much more powerful when it is coupled with expertise.

When executive leaders hire my team to work with their organizations, they usually come with a list of problems for us to solve. As they describe their challenges, one of the first questions we ask them is, "What is the purpose of this particular activity or project? What are you trying to accomplish through your actions?" More often than not, the reaction we get from the leaders is a moment of silence and a thoughtful stare, followed by a response like "You know, that is a really great question. I haven't really thought about it actively in that way—I just wanted my team to make something happen."

I worked with one customer whose team created and designed a brochure about their services, and when it came time to decide how to print and distribute it, he called me, frustrated and concerned that his team had not delivered what he wanted. When I asked what the brochure was intended to accomplish, the response was, "I'm not sure." In other words, his team had wasted valuable time, energy, and money creating something without understanding what is was for—and to add salt to the wound, the design work had been assigned to someone lacking in marketing expertise. It was no surprise to me that the document had not met expectations. It had not been created from a position of strength, so the results were less than powerful. In the days that followed, I worked with the team to clarify the purpose of the brochure and to ensure that the most skilled person on the team actually created the design. As strength (in terms of intention and skill set) was applied to this small project, the outcome was successful: a well-designed brochure that met the business's needs.

Keep things moving.

Speed is just as important to power as strength. Too often, we get side-tracked by performing intense due diligence and analytics before we ever take action. I am not suggesting acting with no research or evaluation; however, I am suggesting understanding when enough is enough. This means that at some point your team must move out of *planning* to make a decision or take an action—otherwise known as analysis paralysis—and into *doing*.

One of the simplest yet most overlooked ways to make forward progress is to make a list of all the actions that are required to get you from start to finish on a particular task or project. This is kind of like the to-do lists many of us create in our personal lives. It's always amazing to me how I can go for weeks thinking about, needing to, or wanting to finish some activity or project around the house, and as soon as I write down what I need to do, the task seems to get completed!

This same phenomenon plays out with companies and teams. Some leaders start to feel like hamsters running on a wheel, moving faster and faster and yet getting nowhere. When I work with people who feel this way and ask them to show me a list of their tasks or things that need to get done, I generally hear something like "I don't have a list; it's all in my head" or "I have so much on my plate, I don't even know where to start." I always respond the same way: "The best place to start is to move it out of your head and onto paper." I like to brainstorm with these leaders to come up with a list of things they believe need to be accomplished. I don't ask them to write them down in order of importance or logical order; I simply request the free flow of ideas. And as the ideas start popping, their action list begins to take shape.

Once the individual I'm working with feels he or she has created an exhaustive list of the tasks that need to be accomplished, we then begin the process of assigning the workload. There is no such thing as a perfect moment to make a change or the perfect solution to a problem. This is one of the easiest power actions you can apply with your team right now. If you sense any inactivity or lack of progress on a particular goal, decision, or project, ask for a meeting. Ask your team members to tell you every step they think they need to take to complete a task. As they share their ideas, have yourself or an assigned scribe write or type their thoughts. Let each person finish offering all their thoughts before you offer insight or ask further questions. With a list of all the to-do items in front of you, you and your team can now assign priorities, dates, and owners for each of the actions. In other words, moving ideas from the head to paper is a catalyst for moving from thinking to doing!

Maintain your progress.

Just like training our bodies to be physically fit and powerful requires consistency and improvement, so does using power wisely in business practices. Being powerful is not a one-time event or a one-time application of brute force; it requires maintenance. This means that strength and speed must be part of the culture and DNA of the organization.

How do you do this with your team? It's simple. Strength is maintained by encouraging your team to consistently ask and verify the purpose for the decisions that are made and the actions that are taken. When I recommend this ask-and-verify technique to managers, the normal reaction is something like "You're asking my team to question everything?" and my answer is, "Absolutely." Empowering individuals to ask if their current actions are still meeting the needs of the business, or if they have gotten stale and need a bit of an overhaul, is one of the best ways I have discovered to maintain strength in an organization. When an organization or an individual takes the same action over and over again, the power can get stagnant, and when this happens, it's time to make a change.

Progress does not stop at just knowing a change has been made; it only happens when the people with the right skill sets are assigned to make it happen. In addition, the speed at which the change gets made is critical to maintaining progress. You can't move your car forward without stepping on the gas pedal, and you can't take any action in business without a swift push in the right direction. Once a decision is made, take action quickly, and refrain from too much debate and analysis.

With the right mix of strength and speed, you will create and sustain results for you and your organization—and you will know you're using your power wisely.

Using Power Wisely in Action

Deborah, a seasoned project manager, was asked by her senior manager to take over a business initiative to improve the customer order processing cycle. This particular program had been struggling for a while, and a number of people had tried and failed to make any forward progress with it.

In an attempt to learn from her predecessors' experience, Deborah began the project by scouring through the previous action lists, project updates, and progress reports they had created. As she scanned through the various templates, e-mails, and project worksheets, Deborah was frustrated to discover that there was nothing readily available that described the initial purpose of the project. As she continued to search through the mountains of paper and electronic files, the only thing that closely resembled a purpose for the program was an e-mail from Matthew, the director of the order management department, to the previous project leader, which stated, "Our customers are complaining about their orders taking too long to be processed, and some have expressed concern that their orders have been lost by my team. Something is clearly wrong, and I need it fixed right away." That was it—the only record that Deborah could find that remotely resembled a goal or desired outcome for the project.

As she continued to dig, she found an enormous amount of e-mail traffic between the previous project managers and the IT team. The e-mails between these two groups were full of pointed accusations about inadequate system functionalities, lack of proper user training, and lack of proper planning on IT's part. As Deborah read through the e-mails, it was clear that the cause of the reported problems was the implementation of a series of system software updates that had occurred six months earlier. IT's stance was that this system upgrade had been designed to improve the order processing time previously reported to them by the order management team, but based on the string of very frustrated and heated e-mails between Matthew, Deborah's predecessors, and IT, it was obvious their solution had not only failed to solve the original issue but had actually created *more* issues. The infighting between IT and the order management team was preventing everyone from moving toward their goal: improving the customer order cycle time.

It was no wonder the program had failed so many times. The IT team had clearly tried to create a solution that would fix the problem, but they had done so without a solid understanding of the desired outcome. So IT thought that they had implemented a great innovation, and order management was furious that their workflow had declined because of this change—which only made IT defensive. The improvement project was at a standstill.

With all the bad blood surrounding this project, Deborah knew she needed to start with a clean slate. She went to Matthew to gather more information about the problem, but it quickly became apparent that he did not understand, or even care to understand, the problem. He just wanted the problem fixed, and he seemed to think that he could make that happen simply by wielding his power.

As a seasoned project manager, Deborah knew she had to create a sound intention for the program if she was going to succeed in fixing the problem at hand, so she asked Matthew for permission to discuss the issues with his team, and he agreed. After a few sessions with the managers responsible for taking customer orders, Deborah uncovered why they were experiencing delays: The system automatically placed orders on hold if there was no quote number entered on the order. This automatic hold was designed to ensure that the order the customer placed matched the quote, and it was supposed to decrease the order management validation time by up to thirty minutes per order—but the reality was that very few customers sent that information with their orders, which meant that most orders were being placed on hold until a quote number was entered. In order to secure that number, the order management representative had to call the customer to ask for the quote number, and in many instances the customer had to contact their internal salesperson to get that information—all of which took a lot of time. So, as it turned out, this system change, which was supposed to decrease processing time, was actually increasing it to the point that the majority of customer orders were being delayed by a minimum of one to two days.

With this detailed information, Deborah was able to create a clear intention for improvement: to decrease the quote validation process from two days to less than thirty minutes. She quickly created a team of order managers and IT individuals and asked them to brainstorm a list of actions they needed to take to solve the problem.

The first few minutes of the session were a disaster. The team members, many of whom had been on the previous project, began rehashing the same blame-game details Deborah had witnessed in her predecessors' notes and e-mail chains. Several of them told Deborah they refused to offer any more input until someone figured out why the issues had happened in the first place. Seeing that her team was in danger of getting stuck in analysis paralysis, Deborah calmly stopped the conversation and said, "Let's keep our focus on the intention. We need to improve our order entry process for quoted orders from two days to less than thirty minutes. Let's discuss the actions that need to happen to get us to meet that goal instead of dwelling on how we got here." She reminded her team that fighting with one another would not create either positive or forward progress, and she encouraged them to remember that the best way to move toward their goal was to take action—not to rehash old wounds. She assured the group that they would measure their progress along the way, and that changes could be implemented quickly as needed.

Many people on the team still seemed apprehensive after listening to what Deborah had to say, but they all agreed to move ahead. Together, they began brainstorming ways to improve the quote validation process. After one week of collaborating on a solution, both IT and order management felt they had an option that would work. IT created a design document, order management reviewed it, and as these actions were completed, the team felt they were finally headed toward improvement. Their focus and energy shifted from blaming to excitement in reaching their goals. Within six months, the program that had been stalled for over two years was running smoothly. Matthew was ecstatic with the results. Deborah had used her power wisely, and her actions had paid off!

People Leadership Action Steps to Using Power Wisely

1. Describe how your team uses power. What practices make them most powerful?

2. Come up with some steps you can take to use power wisely in every task, decision, or project in which you engage.

3. Think about a time when you saw power used wisely. What made it successful?

"Leadership is the wise use of power. Power is the capacity to translate intention into reality and sustain it."

—Warren G. Bennis

16

Practice Risk Acceptance

Risk is one of those situations that many of us try to avoid at all costs. We feel more comfortable taking the proven route or making safe decisions. Driven by a desire to succeed, we hesitate to engage in activities that might lead to poor performance or failure. But the greatest successes of all time have come from people having the courage to take huge risks. Think of Martin Luther King, Jr. He risked his life every day to spread his vision and dream for civil rights in the United States. What if he had woken up one day and said, "There are people out there who don't like my message. It might be dangerous for me to go out and speak today. I think I'll just stay inside." If King had not had made tough decisions every day, the civil rights movement might have had a very different outcome. His risks paid off for an entire nation, and to this day, his efforts are seen as heroic and inspiring.

Leading people in the workplace requires acceptance of risk. Practicing risk acceptance means:

- Operating outside of the fishbowl.
- Testing the waters and adjusting.
- Finding the good in any outcome.

Operate outside of the fishbowl.

There's a story about a goldfish who travelled with a county fair and lived inside of a very small glass bowl. Every day, the fish merrily swam in small circles around his tiny fish bowl. He loved swimming and watching the strange activities that went on around him.

One day, a young boy threw a Ping-Pong ball into the glass bowl and won the fish as a prize. The boy, ecstatic because he finally had a fish for his new aquarium, dumped the fish into the large tank as soon as he got home from the fair. He watched in anticipation, waiting for the fish to swim around the entire aquarium. Instead he noticed that it swam in very small circles. *Hmm, that's weird*, he thought. *Guess the fish is just scared. It will be better tomorrow.*

Day after day, the boy came back hoping to see the fish swimming across the entire tank, and every day, the fish continued to swim in the same small circles. Those small circles represented the environment that it was used to living in—the small fishbowl it had lived in during its time at the county fair. And it refused to venture outside of that environment to see what lay beyond.

Many of us are similar to the goldfish in this story. We get so accustomed to doing things a certain way that when there is a change in our surroundings, we're scared to venture outside the boundaries we understand. We are reluctant to try anything new or foreign.

Practicing risk acceptance requires encouraging people to operate outside of the fishbowl. The first step to doing this is to provide a safe space into which they can venture. I hear from many leaders that "people can't change," but the truth is, they can—they just need guidance in trying new ideas and ways of operating, an opportunity to see situations differently. People leaders give their team members the permission to take risks, brainstorm new ideas, and question everything with the attitude that change might be beneficial. If the young boy in that story had pushed the fish a little outside its small circle each day, the fish might have realized that it had a whole new world awaiting it.

Test the waters and adjust.

When you get into the shower, do you turn on the water and then jump right in? Probably not, unless you want to freeze or scald yourself! Most likely you test the water before you put your whole body in. If it is too cold, you add a little hot; it if is too hot, you add a little cold; and you keep testing and adjusting until the water temperature is just right.

It's much easier to take risks when you've allowed yourself to test the waters first. In business, this means trying out a new idea or solution before you implement it full-scale. I've led and participated in hundreds of change initiatives and projects in my lifetime, and each time, the thing that has made the difference in whether they have succeeded or failed has been my team's willingness to take risks. Those members that wanted to evaluate every potential negative action or reaction with their program and make sure problems were resolved before the project proceeded were the first to fall short, because they either missed deadlines or overspent budgets. In trying to design a perfect, safe, no-problems solution, the team lost its effectiveness. Most of these projects were cancelled because the team was too scared to move into action. When this happened, it was a huge waste of our team's valuable time and our organization's money.

In my experience, "perfect" only exists in minds and on paper. The only way to make something progress forward is to come up with a solution that is good enough and then test it. It takes trust—and guts—for a team to move out of analysis paralysis, and as a leader, it's your job to create a culture of risk acceptance within your team. You can do this by giving your employees permission to try out their ideas with the full understanding something may not work as expected.

When a new idea gets put into motion, watch carefully for any hiccups. If any disruptions occur, make quick tweaks and adjustments until the kinks work themselves out. Once you feel the process is working as expected, it can be implemented on a larger scale.

Find the good.

No matter how good your idea is, how well you plan, or how well you test, something is probably going to go wrong at some point. We all know about Murphy's Law—"what can go wrong will go wrong"—and while I see this as a pessimistic view of the world, unfortunately, it can be very true at times. And one big reason people are scared to accept and take risks is because of the consequence attached to failing. All too often, I've seen leaders challenge and push their teams to take risks and then chastise their staff for doing a poor job if the project or action does not turn out as expected.

I have been on the receiving end of this treatment, and I can assure you, this type of behavior only makes you want to play it small and safe going forward. As a people leader practicing risk acceptance, you must be poised and ready to accept any outcome. This means that you look for the good in everything that happens as a result of taking that risk.

When you start looking for the good in every situation that results from taking a risk, you will see that it is not hard to find. If nothing else, at least your team had the strength to move through their fears and take the risk. That on its own is a huge success. You may also find that the perceived failure actually uncovers an issue that would have caused future problems if you had not ventured forward with the change—or maybe you'll discover an antiquated practice that has no value and save your company thousands of dollars by getting rid of it. Finding good in any problem is not hard to do; you just have to look for it.

When you practice risk acceptance in your team, you create a culture and environment in which it is safe to exceed expectations. In this kind of space, your team will feel more empowered and engaged, and their productivity will soar.

Practicing Risk Acceptance in Action

Adelaide was the distribution manager for a large warehouse operation. Out of three other major warehouses in the company, hers produced service metrics to the customers at the lowest cost to the company. Adelaide was proud of her team's performance. Their success had come from continuously improving their processes and systems to meet the increases in customer demands. However, with budget cuts and continued demands to decrease the workforce, Adelaide was concerned that her team's outstanding results were about to take a turn for the worse—something that made her particularly nervous because the executives were breathing down her neck every day, expecting her to continue to produce more work with fewer resources.

Frustrated and flustered by the situation, Adelaide knew she and her team had to implement something dramatically different in their day-to-day operations to meet her superiors' expectations. She needed some new and fresh ideas, so she began holding small sessions with her team members to get their input on opportunities for change.

When they started brainstorming, Adelaide immediately noticed how defeated her team was. "There is nothing we can do," they told her. "We are doing the best with what we've got. Management just doesn't understand."

After listening to her team for a while, Adelaide said, "I realize that based on reality right now, it seems we cannot get any better. However, let's pretend that we can. Let's imagine that we can do anything we want to change our circumstances. If we had a blank canvas and an unlimited amount of resources, what would we do?"

After a bit of silence, a few team members began spouting off ideas. "I wish we had a new warehouse system. Ours is too slow. If they want us to get the work done, they need to give us more people, and we need to get rid of the people that aren't pulling their weight."

Adelaide's team members' comments weren't bad, but they were obvious, tried-and-true solutions that had worked for them in the past. She realized she needed to challenge them in a different way to get new ideas out of them, so she asked, "What would you do if you knew you couldn't fail?"

The room went silent, and her team looked at her like she had just spoken in a foreign language.

"I know this is different than previous requests," Adelaide said. "But I am giving you permission to bring any idea to me for consideration, even if you think it sounds crazy or impossible." At the end of the meeting, she encouraged her staff to keep the ideas percolating and flowing throughout the week.

As Adelaide walked the warehouse floor over the next week, it was obvious that creativity was in full force. Not only did she notice a higher morale, she also found that her group's productivity seemed to be increasing, even though no big changes had even been implemented. It was as if just by urging her team to think differently and giving them permission to try new things without a major consequence for their actions she had lifted an enormous pressure off their shoulders. The fear of making change that had been so pervasive in the warehouse's culture was beginning to be replaced with the attitude of "We'll never know until we try!"

At first Adelaide's team began with small changes, like changing the location of the most frequently picked items on orders to increase the efficiency of the orders each day. With each successful change, however, the team got bolder—and after watching the workflow for a few weeks, they brought forward their most risky recommendation yet. They told Adelaide that inventory receiving and replenishing was happening during the day at the same time the main order picking and shipping volume was happening. Because of this activity, there was a lot of congestion in the aisles of the warehouse. Not only did this cause delays in completing customer orders, it was also unsafe for the people on the warehouse floor. In order to streamline the workflow and make the environment safer, they recommended that the receiving and replenishment activities be performed on a third shift.

This was a radical and risky idea, and Adelaide was concerned that her director would not approve of it—but before she told her team "no," she went and reviewed the third-shift concept with upper management. To her surprise, they told her that as long as she did not have to hire more people or increase payroll expenses, her team was free to implement the change.

Adelaide shared the good news with her team members, who promptly put the plan in place: five of the individuals from the day shift changed their hours to the newly created third shift, which meant they would be working from ten at night until six in the morning of the next day. The new shift team quickly realized there was more work to do than they thought, however. Five of them could not consistently stock all of the product needed for the next day's work. Because of this understaffing, customer orders were being delayed in the picking process, which was resulting in a decline of the warehouse's overall delivery performance.

When this decline began to show up in the daily metrics report, upper management told Adelaide to stop the third shift and go back to the way things were before the change. She was tempted to take the easy way out and go back to where they had been, but she had promised her team that they would try this new system for a month, and it had only been a few days so far. She decided to hold a meeting with the third-shift staff to get their view on the issues.

"Tell me one good thing we have learned in implementing this shift change," Adelaide said at the beginning of the meeting. Her staff thought she was crazy. "There is nothing good, we just screwed up," they told her. "It doesn't work. We need to go back to the way things were before." However, Adelaide was not going to let them give up on themselves so easily. She continued to probe into the reasons why the third shift was struggling. When the team reached the consensus that they needed more resources to complete the work, Adelaide found some more employees who were willing to move from their current day-shift position to the third-shift hours.

Less than two weeks after the newly revised third-shift team began operating, the results of the change started impacting the overall warehouse performance in a positive manner. Customer orders were flowing out the door more quickly and with less cost than before the third-shift idea was implemented, and the first- and second-shift teams were able to work more productively, with fewer bottlenecks and delays than they'd had before the change.

Adelaide was extremely proud to see these kind of results from her team, who'd originally said it couldn't be done. If they had not taken the risk of creating the new shift and working out the kinks, the warehouse performance would have stayed the same, and her team would have felt like they had failed. Instead, in practicing risk acceptance with her team, they figured out a creative way to be more effective and productive.

People Leadership Action Steps to Practicing Risk Acceptance

1. Think about your leadership approach. How do you encourage your team to live outside their fish bowl?

2. When your team makes risky changes, do they jump right in or try it out first? Think about how you can create an environment that encourages testing out new ideas.

3. Think about a situation in which you took a risk and were successful. How did you feel? What support did you have from your leadership to take the risk?

"If you risk nothing, then you risk everything."

—Geena Davis

17
Give Credit; Accept Blame

There is a simple way to measure the strength of a people leader when it comes to giving credit and accepting blame—a simple test that works on any leader, regardless of his or her title, position, or rank. All you have to do is count the number of times he or she uses the word "I" when describing something positive or outstanding, and the number of times he or she uses the words "you" or "the team" when talking about a problem or failure. Are the leader's comments full of "I was very happy with the results; I pushed the team really hard to do their best, and I gave them everything they needed to get the job done"? Or does the leader humbly respond, "The team's efforts really paid off; their dedication and passion is what made the difference"? And equally as important, if not more so, what words does the leader choose when the proverbial shit hits the fan and results are poor or fall short of expectations? Does the leader say things like "I was responsible for the mistakes that were made—the team did a great job"? Or does he or she rant, "The team had everything they needed to be successful and they failed; they never told me there were any problems"? If the "I" wins when giving credit, the leader is more focused on him or herself than on his or her people. And when blame is handed out to "the team," you can be sure that the leader is attempting to save face.

Effective people leaders give credit and accept blame by:

- Keeping their egos in check.
- Showcasing the team's efforts.
- Accepting responsibility for failures.

Keep your ego in check.

As I have shared in previous chapters, many people are motivated by recognition. After all, it feels really good when someone gives us kudos for doing a great job. And society teaches us at a very young age that in order to win or succeed, we must do our best, even at the expense of others. This is the basis of any competition, whether in sports, music, or even intellectual challenges. In order for there to be a winner, there must be a loser. So we work hard through our formative years to make our marks on our personal worlds.

Unfortunately, over time, this personal drive to win often feeds this nasty little part of our character called our ego—which I think of as a little devil always cheering us on to do anything we can to make ourselves look good and the people around us to look just a little bit worse. We all have an ego, of course, and to a certain extent, we need it to survive; the key, though, is how we allow it to function in our lives.

Personally, my ego really thrives on being right. No matter whom I encounter or what situation I tackle, my first instinct is to design the circumstances in such a way that I can be the genius in the end. When I first began my career, I received many financial incentives and promotions by making smart decisions and showing people that my ideas would help my team succeed. After I began managing people, however, I quickly discovered that in order for me to get my way and be the brilliant star I wanted to be, someone that was part of my team had to suffer. In my efforts to protect myself, I was actually responsible for more than one of my team members losing their jobs.

Over time, this way of behaving really started eating away at me internally. When I achieved or exceeded my goals, I no longer got the high I'd gotten in the past. I was frustrated, stressed, and burned out. I got tired of having to always be right. So—out of sheer exhaustion—I slowly and surely started asking for help from my team. I encouraged my employees to take on more responsibilities and make more decisions, and I mentored them to achieve their goals. I had to shift my focus away from my need to be right and toward working with my team to support them in their success—and believe me, this took some time to master—but eventually I made the change.

Just like breaking any bad habit, consistency is all it takes to keep your ego in check. In my case, I first had to let go of that ingrained belief that being successful could only come from my actions. This required me to step out on the faith that my needs would be met when I enabled others to exceed. Ultimately, I found that constantly reminding myself that people leadership was not all about me but rather about the people around me was the best way to ensure my ego stayed in check.

Showcase your team.

As a leader, those outside of your immediate organization—your peers, your customers, your superiors—will often give you credit for your team's successes. No matter how tempting (and seemingly harmless) it might be to simply accept the kudos, it is important to make sure your team is given the credit they deserve. This may be difficult at first, but after a while, you will find that your desire for others' success will drive you to give the team credit for the work with no mention of your efforts, even in those times when you have personally played a big part.

Besides feeling energized inside, there are two amazing outcomes that you will personally experience when you showcase your team's efforts. First, when you acknowledge your team's hard work, they will be willing to work more diligently and effectively than you can imagine. Their internal spark will be ignited knowing that they are being seen for the effort that they are giving to the organization, and it will drive them to give even more. Second, people will begin to view your team as the trusted experts and go-getters in the company, which will make your department invaluable. There are no guarantees of job security in this day and age—but having a reputation as a valued expert is the closest thing you can get to it.

Accept responsibility for failures.

Just as important as showcasing your team's talents is protecting them from having their reputations tainted by failure. I have seen far too many managers dish out the compliments and then throw the daggers at the first sign of a troubled performance. I've even seen it in pro football: a team loses a game, and the coach tells the media that he had a great game plan that the team simply failed to execute—and when the team comes out the next week, they perform even more poorly and lose again. In those instances when a coach says, "My team played tough and gave it their all; I should have had a better game plan," on the other hand, the team is inspired to play harder, and they usually do better the next week.

Remember, you are a people leader—and that means it's important for you to be willing to "take one on the chin" for your team once in a while. This does not mean that you shouldn't do your proper due diligence to determine what went wrong, of course. Whether there was a communication failure, a misalignment of expectations between you and a key employee, or any other issue, find the source of the problem or cause for the failure and work it out so it does not happen again. But don't place public blame on anyone. Doing so leaves the person completely embarrassed and deflated. When your team sees you watching out for them by accepting responsibility for their mistakes, in contrast, they will feel empowered— and their loyalty to you will only increase, which will make them want to keep you from looking bad in the future.

Giving credit and accepting blame is just one more proven way to establish trust with your team. The more your team feels your support, the more they will respond with their increased effectiveness and productivity.

Giving Credit and Accepting Blame in Action

In a major operations project to relocate warehouses, Betty was the team member responsible for representing the department that purchased the inventory of product that was going to be housed in the facility. Her job was to make sure the move did not negatively impact the purchasing team's workload or workflow.

Jan, the project manager, had advised Betty's manager to have her hold sessions with each purchasing agent on her team to find out what his or her needs and concerns were—but on the weekly team project calls, when Jan asked her project leaders for their updates, Betty's updates were short and offered very few details. Jan had worked with the purchasing team in the past, and they had always been very vocal and forthcoming with their opinions, so she was confused by how little information Betty was offering up. She arranged to speak separately with Betty about the quality of her updates, and when they spoke, she discovered that Betty had not gone to the purchasing team for input at all; she just assumed her personal insights would be good enough.

As Jan continued their conversation by asking Betty detailed questions about the process, Betty realized she had made a mistake. She promised Jan that she would contact each of her purchasing counterparts to get his or her feedback on the project and provide a thorough update on the next project team call.

At the next team call, Jan asked Betty for an update on behalf of the purchasing team. This time Betty shared a few ideas, but not nearly as many as Jan expected. Jan could feel her temper rising out of the top of her head. She was ready to come through the phone. *What part of my instructions can't Betty understand?* she fumed. *Is she stupid? I am so sick and tired of having to ask her for the same thing over and over again. Why can't she get this?*

Jan was tempted to address the issue right there and then, but something inside of her encouraged her to hold her tongue. She knew that erupting at this point and blaming Betty for her poor performance would only cause more delays to the team. So she waited until the call was over, and then she reached out to Betty separately again. As they talked, Jan realized that Betty really did not grasp her role. Betty said she wasn't comfortable talking to the purchasing team about the project because she was uncertain what questions to ask them. Her manager had told her to make the calls but hadn't given her any direction as to how she needed to represent the team.

Bingo! Jan had uncovered the issue. *Thank goodness I did not make Betty look stupid for doing a poor job*, she thought. *I didn't communicate in detail what we expected. I assumed that had been done by her manager.* With that moment of clarity, Jan admitted to Betty that she was to blame for the confusion, and the two of them continued their discussion until Betty clearly understood what she needed to get from the purchasing team.

At the next project update, Betty confidently shared her team's feedback. She even pointed out a few flaws in the project plan actions and timelines which were adjusted prior to the first product move. Jan could have said, "You know, Betty, the only reason you were able to provide this insight is because I pointed you in the right direction. You weren't getting this until I stepped in. We could have had a major disaster on our hands." Instead, she honored Betty for her efforts and invaluable feedback. And that was all Betty needed: some clarity and some credit for a job well done.

The warehouse move went on with only a few minor glitches. When it was done, it was considered one of the smoothest projects implemented in the operations team. And Betty stayed very engaged and supportive throughout the entire project—all because Jan kept her own ego in check and gave Betty credit where credit was due.

People Leadership Action Steps to Giving Credit and Accepting Blame

1. Think of a time when you felt your ego controlling your interactions with your team. How did it make you feel? How did your team react?

2. Reflect on a time when you showcased another team member's efforts. How did they respond? How did it make you feel?

3. When something goes wrong on your team, who accepts the responsibility? Come up with some steps you can take to assume more responsibility for your teams' actions.

"A good leader is a person who takes a little more than his share of the blame and a little less than his share of the credit."

—John C. Maxwell

18
Address Difficult Team Members Immediately

No one likes dealing with difficult people. They come in various forms— arrogant know-it-alls who refuse to acknowledge anyone's ideas except their own, perpetual whiners who complain about everything, slackers who never meet their deadlines or who always have an excuse when they fail to follow through on their commitments. No matter what their negative traits are, interacting with difficult people can drain you of all of your energy or leave you feeling frustrated and at your wits' end—so, rather than confronting them, most of us avoid these hard-to-deal-with people like the plague. However, when challenging individuals are left to their own devices, they become the plague of your organization; through his or her presence alone, one difficult person can wipe out an entire team's effectiveness.

People leaders must deal with difficult people on their teams before their antagonistic behaviors cultivate gargantuan problems in their entire department. Allowing troublesome habits to fester in one person contributes to the loss of productivity of the entire team. Your other team members will waste hours of valuable work time avoiding the challenging individual and complaining unendingly about your inability to deal with that person. Furthermore, if your strong team members get fed up with your lack of action, they may lose respect for your leadership abilities and decide to quit—or, even worse, join forces with the difficult people.

Addressing difficult team members effectively requires:

- Acknowledging the issue.
- Addressing the behavior rather than attacking the person.
- Getting to the root of the problem and creating a solution.
- Improving or moving on.

Acknowledge the issue.

Oftentimes it seems like the safest and easiest way to deal with a problem is to ignore it and hope it will go away. But imagine if the Apollo 13 crew had ignored the issues with the oxygen tank in the spaceship instead of acknowledging, "Houston, we have a problem?" The entire crew would have been killed.

The stakes may not be quite as high at work, but sticking your head in the sand and pretending an issue is not there, or even just giving it to another leader to solve, is a surefire recipe for disaster. When you witness or hear of any unacceptable behaviors or actions within your team, then, the first thing to do is acknowledge it. Doing so means that at the first inkling or sign of a bad situation, you gather the facts and have a conversation with the person who appears to be the problem child.

When you talk to the person who is creating the problem, it's critical that your discussion be levelheaded and non-accusatory, and that it includes a good representation of factual examples—no matter how frustrated, angry, or disappointed you might be. If you prefer to avoid conflict, as many of us do, this action on your part will require courage, confidence, and patience. However, it is an absolute necessity if you want to nip a potential problem in the bud before it turns into a poisonous growth in your team.

Target the behavior, not the person.

As you are discussing the problem with your team member, ensure that you confront the unacceptable behavior—but don't make a personal attack on the team member's character. We all have our own judgments and labels, conscious and subconscious, but it's critical to set these aside when dealing with difficult team members because it creates a barrier that is hard to penetrate when trying to solve a problem with an individual. For instance, if a person is habitually late to work, conference calls, and meetings, my frustration with his or her behaviors may cause me to label him or her as a lazy, unreliable, or slacker employee—but in doing so, I remove any opportunity for the employee to improve or better his or her performance. When addressing difficult team members, therefore, it is critical to begin with a positive, neutral, and open mindset.

The most effective way to address hard-to-deal-with people is to discuss the behaviors they've been displaying or actions they've been taking that are inappropriate or unacceptable. Stick with the facts: offer constructive feedback about the individual's actions, and highlight the consequences his or her behaviors are producing for the rest of the team. When providing this constructive criticism, remember what Mary Poppins taught us: "A spoonful of sugar helps the medicine go down." With this in mind, an effective way to address a late employee might be to say, "I have noticed that you have gotten to work ten to fifteen minutes late every day for the last ten days in a row. I've also noticed that you've been arriving at least five minutes late to every meeting or conference call. We miss your valuable input when you're not there; we really benefit from you being on time."

After you share your comments, stop talking and listen. Give your team member time and space to respond. You may discover that the team member is not happy about his or her behavior either but doesn't know how to fix it and needs your help to find a solution. On some rare occasions, the person may simply admit to having behaved poorly. Sometimes he or she is simply testing the waters to see how long he or she can get away with poor performance. Regardless of why they're doing what they're doing, when you address difficult employees' behavior without attacking them personally, they will be more likely to hear your concerns and want to improve.

Get to the root of the problem and create a solution.

Simply pointing out your concern about an employee's problematic behavior is not enough to create a long-lasting change in performance. For real improvement to take place, you must create a solution that works for you, your team member, and your team as a whole. Idle threats and demands to "do better" do not lead to long-lasting, effective results. I encourage you to get to the root of the situation in order to create a solution that will stick.

We are not born to be persnickety. Being difficult is a learned behavior that generally stems from one of two things: fear or stress. When people act out, it's often because they are scared of looking stupid or fearful of not being accepted. Stress also contributes to bad behavior at work: Maybe the person is late to work because one of his children always forgets her homework and he sacrifices being on time to prevent his child from getting in trouble at school. Or maybe she's being extra snappy and demanding at work because she just found out a loved one has a terminal illness. The list of contributors to negative behavior is endless; the point is, you need to get to the root cause and then co-create a solution with the team member in question.

To create improvement, ask your employee his or her ideas and thoughts about how his or her actions could positively change. Encourage the person to offer insights into how he or she can resolve the problem. If the team member asks for input, or if he or she appears to be struggling for ideas, offer some solutions of your own. The key is to work together *with* the team member to develop an action plan that will deliver long-lasting results. Document the plan with the expected actions, outcomes, and timelines by which the behavior will be improved, and then agree to move forward with the plan.

Improve or move on.
The last step in addressing difficult team members is to make sure that their behavior improves. Once an action plan for improvement is established, it's essential to hold regular check-ins and follow-ups with the employee. As you see positive changes taking place, recognize the team member for his or her efforts. If, on the other hand, progress is not happening as expected, address your concerns with the employee immediately. Encourage the team member to share about his or her lack of improvement, and offer guidance and support in implementing the changes.

Some behavior changes take longer than others, and as long as there is positive momentum of some sort, continue to work toward the agreed-upon plan. If it becomes clear after several attempts at improvement that the behavior has not changed at all and will most likely not change, however, it is time to make a different decision. At this point, it may be advisable to seek guidance from your human resources or executive team about how to remove this employee from your team and organization. Sometimes it is better for everyone, including the difficult team member, to stop fighting the issue and move on.

Addressing difficult employees swiftly and consistently establishes the tone not only for the employees in question but also for the rest of your team. When your employees see how you deal with negative actions and behaviors, they will know that you are willing to confront problems, and you will win their respect.

Addressing Difficult Team Members Immediately in Action

Sonny, Vice President of operations, was conducting a search to fill an open director role in his organization. He knew he had to be particularly careful in choosing the candidate for the position because he'd recently moved the previous director into another department due to his inability to deliver on key business objectives and performance goals. Whatever candidate was selected was going to have to implement changes that would immediately improve overall performance of the order management team and increase the current customer service levels within the department.

Sonny interviewed a few internal candidates, but ultimately he felt that the order management team would benefit from someone with an outside perspective. After a lengthy selection process, Sonny and his executive team decided to hire Hardy. They felt his previous experience in various operational departments, as well as the list of accomplishments on his resume, were impressive, and that he would be a great fit for the position.

Hardy jumped right into his new role, telling the staff that he had been hired to improve the performance of the order management department and—like a bull in a china shop—making his presence known by shattering current processes and systems, not to mention chastising people for what he perceived to be ineffective work. Hardy spent no time assessing or reviewing what was working or not working in the department's day-to-day operations; he simply insisted that what he had done in the past would work best to improve his new staff's performance. He expected his team to accomplish immediate change by implementing the policies and procedures that had been successful in his previous company, no questions asked.

Unbeknownst to Hardy, his demands were falling on deaf ears. His tone of communicating and his dictatorial behavior initiated more dysfunction and chaos than had existed before he was hired. The managers were unclear as to why anything in their department needed to improve. No one, including Sonny, had communicated concerns or inadequacies within the order management department—and their previous director had been moved out of his position so quickly that the staff was still in a state of confusion over what had gone awry with him. Unsure of what was happening, and frustrated with Hardy's tactics, the order managers spent most of their time complaining to one another—and sometimes even to the customers— about the mess Hardy was creating. Productivity went down, and nobody was happy.

Several employees courageously approached Hardy to share their frustrations with his leadership style and behavior—but he refused to listen to them and accused them of being whiners, resistant to change. He reminded them (again) that the executives had hired him for his expertise and that they all simply needed to comply and conform to his requests for improvement.

From that point forward, the Order Management team's overall performance and productivity took a nosedive. Employees consistently began missing work or showing up late. Important goals and deadlines were not being met. The staff's frustrations with Hardy began showing up in their attitudes at work and treatment of customers, which led to an increase in customer complaints.

When Sonny approached Hardy with these customer concerns, he immediately pled his case and defended himself by telling Sonny that the order managers were unwilling to work to make positive change happen. : Sonny directed Hardy to continue to push through the team's resistance and to quickly make positive progress in performance—so instead of changing his tactics, Hardy pushed his team harder than ever before.

Utter chaos was raging through the order management department. Feeling like she was at her wits' end, one of the order management supervisors approached Gemma, a trusted leader in the operations department, for advice and help with the Hardy situation. The manager explained how Hardy was causing order managers undue stress and strain, which was causing productivity and morale to plummet in the department. After hearing her out, Gemma volunteered, as an objective third-party observer, to discuss the issues with Hardy and the order management team with Sonny. She had worked with Sonny before, so she felt comfortable approaching him with their concerns.

Gemma went to Sonny and explained to him that Hardy was trying to force-fit change to critical business processes and procedures with no understanding of the business's or customers' needs. She described the manner in which Hardy was addressing employees, and she told Sonny it was her opinion that the team's performance was rapidly declining because of Hardy's leadership style. Sonny listened, thanked Gemma for sharing her concerns, and assured her that he would address the situation with Hardy immediately.

Weeks went by, and Hardy's behaviors remained the same. Gemma was continuing to hear nothing but bad news from the order management individuals, and she began to wonder whether Sonny had spoken with Hardy—and if so, what he had said to him. If Sonny had met with Hardy to address his behavior, there was no evidence of it that Gemma could see. Complaints continued to mount, performance continued to decrease, and almost every order manager and supervisor was frustrated and ready to look for a job anywhere where Hardy was not working.

Several weeks later, after hearing again and again that Hardy was still bulldozing over his team members, Gemma approached Sonny again with her concerns and asked him what he'd done to improve the situation. He explained that he had brought the problem to Hardy's attention and directed him to do what was necessary to fix it. As their conversation continued, Gemma realized that Sonny had not addressed the *real* problem: Hardy's behavior. She was frustrated and disappointed that Sonny had offered no insight, input, or direction to Hardy about him—not his team—being the problem.

Disruption in the order management team continued for several more months. The team's performance and service levels declined to an all-time low. When customer complaints reached an all-time high, Sonny was forced to deal with Hardy—but instead of addressing his behavior and working with him to resolve it, he simply moved him to another department. There, Hardy propagated the same issues in his new team as he had with the order management team. Ultimately, in ignoring Hardy's behavior, Sonny created unnecessary havoc in not just one but two of his teams. Tens of thousands of dollars were wasted in productivity loss and customer dissatisfaction during Hardy's reign.

People Leadership Action Steps to Addressing Difficult Team Members Immediately

1. Think about how you currently acknowledge difficult team members.

2. Come up with some steps you can take to get to the root problem behind the difficult team member's behaviors or actions.

3. Think about what you have done to address poor behaviors or attitudes in difficult team members in the past and how you can do even better in the future.

4. Reflect upon a time when you witnessed the successful handling of a difficult team member. How was it done?

"Leaders do not avoid, repress, or deny conflict, but rather see it as an opportunity."

—Warren Bennis

19

Measure with Purpose

Remember the first time you got in the driver's seat of a car? Whether you were five and pretending that you were the grown-up driver or fifteen and just learning to drive, one of the first things you probably noticed were the various displays on the dashboard right above the steering wheel. The parent, relative, friend, or driver's education teacher instructing you most likely told you that each of these displays had its own purpose. For instance, the big display with numbers from 0 to 100-plus is the speedometer and indicates how fast you are driving. And the gauge with a small picture of a thermometer and the letters H and C gives you a sense of how hot your car is running. Then there's the display with an E, F, and fractions in between, which signals how much gas your car still has in its tank. Each of these indicators, your instructor told you, plays an important role in the operation and performance of your car, with each one engineered and designed with a specific purpose in mind.

Just like automobiles, organizations need a dashboard to measure and gauge their performance. And just as each of the dashboard displays in your car has a specific purpose behind it, so too do the metrics and reporting in any organization or company. Simply possessing measurements, facts, and statistics about your business is useless unless there is an understanding of their meaning and of how these facts can be used to identify areas for improvement and growth and drive your performance forward.

When I ask the department managers and executives in companies where I consult about how they measure the performance of their business,

I generally get one of two responses: "We have our profit and loss statement. What more do you need to run a business?" or " We have loads of information and measurements in our business. Where would you like to start?" The first response indicates that the group has virtually no data or performance tracking of any kind in their organization, and the second response suggests that they are overwrought with information—which means they are rarely reviewing it and never using it to improve the state of the business.

You don't need a million measurements to assess the state of your overall business or department and its performance; you just need a few critical ones. Creating measurements with purpose enables you to create and organize key business information so you and your team can keep a focused "eye" on how you are performing and provide indicators for improvement.

Measuring your company's performance with purpose requires:

- Identifying key performance indicators.
- Creating easy-to-produce and easy-to-understand measurements.
- Acting on the information.

Identify key performance indicators.

The best way to create measurements that are useful to you and your team is through identifying key performance indicators, or KPIs. These serve as fundamental data points that show your organization's value to the customers and demonstrate the success of your team's performance in specific areas. In many businesses, revenue and profit/loss statements are the only measurements that exist. While these are important pieces of data, they are not necessarily strong indicators of the operations of an organization. You need revenue statements in order to report to the tax authority and shareholders or to track your company's sales for budgeting purposes, yes—but tracking your revenue alone does not demonstrate your team's overall performance.

KPIs will serve your organization best when there is a well-thought-out purpose and intention behind each one of them. Creating meaningful and effective KPIs can be done using the following process: 1) Thoroughly reviewing your organization's key activities and objectives; 2) Surveying your customers about how your services are important to them; 3) Ensuring your process allows you to capture and calculate the expected indicator value; and 4) Selecting your most meaningful indicators.

The first step to creating useful KPIs is to do a thorough review of the key objectives and critical activities your team performs on a daily or frequent basis. This means that you look at each major function or department in your organization to determine how what they are actually doing can lead you toward meeting your key objectives. Whatever your key objectives are, you want to investigate and identify what key tasks your team is in charge of that will lead to the achievement of those goals. If your goal is to increase new customers, then your key activity may be the number of outbound phone calls your team makes to prospective clients on a daily basis. If your goal is to increase sales per existing customer, maybe the key action is the number of times a sales representative suggests an "upsell" item or service to the customer. I refer to this step as aligning your goals with your organization's real-world activity.

Step two in creating your KPIs turns the focus to the customer. At this point, you have a good idea of your internal needs; now it's time to ask what is most important to your customer with regard to your performance. You can reach out to your customer with a personal phone call or through an automated online survey. The key is that you take the time to ask them what their needs are. After all, without a customer, your organization would not exist.

As you receive feedback from your customers, you may be surprised to find that what is important to them may differ from your key objectives. For instance, many large businesses are focused on a specific date by which they need their product shipped, and this might be an important internal goal for the shipping department. However, in speaking with the customer, you may discover that they simply want to make sure that the product arrives by whatever date you've promised. So from your customer's perspective, it is more important to know the percentage of times you delivered the order on the date that was promised, not the date it was shipped. If you are in the service business, maybe your client simply wants you to show up at a specified time, which means the KPI would be percentage of times that the service person arrived on time to an appointment. Getting a firm grasp of how your customers measure your value is critical to understand in your overall measurement reporting.

With a strong list of the internal and external desired indicators, you must now make sure your process and systems are designed to capture the critical data required to create the data point. Teams frequently come up with great ideas for measurements only to find that when they present them to their technology team for development, critical pieces of information are not captured during the operational process. Consider our example above about delivery by promise date. If, in your order entry process, the promise date is not entered by an order management representative, then your desired indicator will be impossible to create.

In the event that you discover a hole in your process or system design, you must make one of two choices: scrap the desired KPI and create a new one that can be measured in your existing process, or change your process so the important information can be measured.

Once you have verified that your process can support the creation of each of your desired KPIs, it is now time to select the chosen few. The ideal number of measurements depends on the size of your organization and the number of departments or key functions. For planning purposes, a good number of KPIs per department is three to four.

Remember, having too many KPIs is just as bad as having too few. More than four indicators per department generally means there is someone, usually an executive, who believes that simply having information at his or her fingertips makes him or her powerful, so he or she requests mounds of information from the team. These people are what I call data hounds. They love to go sniffing out any data they can find; however, when they get the information, they do nothing positive with it.

Establishing a few but mighty KPIs will empower you and your team to measure how you are performing against internal objectives and demonstrating value to your customers.

Create measurements that are easy to produce and understand.

Now that you have established your mighty few measurements, it is time to produce them in a format that is easy for all individuals on your team to generate and understand. The easiest way to produce KPIs is to have them automatically generated in a reporting database or software tool. This might be something simple, like an Excel spreadsheet, or something a bit more complicated, like a fully integrated Enterprise Resource Planning (ERP) system. Regardless of the tool used, it is critical that the indicators be generated quickly and consistently and with minimal manual intervention. I have seen measurements that require an individual to manually merge three separate automated reports into a spreadsheet and manipulate the data to come up with the final number; this kind of effort is not sustainable for frequent and consistent reporting, which is the goal of collecting data on your KPIs.

Remember, the reported metrics must be easily understood by everyone on your team. If you have created these metrics in the four-step process outlined above, then they will be simple to comprehend because they were created based on current activities and customer needs. Remember, you want your measurements to be useful in identifying tangible areas for improvement—and if your KPIs are too complex, using them to change the course of your business will be too complex as well.

Act on the information.
Once equipped with the proper measurements and reporting, make it useful. Before distributing the information to the world, ask yourself: Who needs to see it, and what will they do with it? If you want your KPIs to drive improvements in your business performance, then your audience is most likely your team members or key leaders in your organization. If you want to use your KPIs to demonstrate your value to your customers, then your customer should be one of the recipients of the information.

When you present the information to the interested party, make sure that each person understands what it means. This requires training on where the core data points originate, how the measurement is calculated, and how the performance indicator is important to measuring the success of the department or business. Without proper background and context for a given measurement, abuse and misuse of information can occur. For instance, a novice salesperson could report the information to his or her customer without understanding the purpose and cause the customer to be confused and alarmed, especially if the data does not look positive on the surface. Before any measurements are shared, make sure that each team member has a firm grasp of the background and value of each key performance indicator.

Finally, make sure you and your team use your KPIs consistently. Producing performance measurements for the sake of producing them and not acting on them is counterproductive. One of the best ways to report measurements that can be acted upon by any team is through the use of a scorecard or a dashboard. This format can be created easily in a spreadsheet and provides a good visual representation of your KPIs. The scorecard consists of top indicators, each of which has been assigned a target value or goal, a current value, and a predetermined indicator scale. The target value represents the target result your team is expected to achieve for the particular metric; the current value is how your team is performing on the performance indicator; and the indicator scale is your team's traffic light—in other words, it represents a green, yellow, or red status for each measurement based on the target value. A green indicator means things are flowing as expected, yellow indicates that something is a bit off and that you should proceed with caution, and red means that you need to stop what you are doing and search for an improvement.

In the graphic below, you will see an example of the scorecard concept. The shading represents green (90%), yellow (4), and red (3). There are three KPIs for an operations group: performance to customer promise date, number of rings to answer a customer's call, and number of days a customer order is on hold. For the first measurement, the goal is 90 percent, and the "actual" (meaning the team's actual performance) is 90 percent. If you're replicating this exercise in your business, give it a green value (by highlighting your report in green). It's green because anything greater than or equal to 90 percent indicates a green value, meaning meeting or exceeding the expectation. In the second measurement, the goal is three rings, and the indicator is yellow because the team is performing at four—meaning that something is off in the process and the team needs to make an adjustment. In the third sample metric, the goal is one day, while the actual is three days—so the indicator is red, showing that the performance is way off track.

When your performance indicators are tracked in a template, as displayed in the graphic below, it is easy for you and your team to see where processes and results in your operations are functioning as expected and where they may need some attention. With this type of information, you can purposefully decide what action steps need to be taken to improve any indicator that is lagging in expectations.

Key Performance Indicators
Operations Group (Example)

	Goal	Actual
Performance to Customer Promise Date	90%	90%
Number of Rings to Answer Customer Call	3	4
Number of Days Customer Order is on Hold	1	3

Teams are more effective and efficient when they are provided with purpose-driven measurements.

Measuring with Purpose in Action

As new Director of Operations, Reginald was expected to continue in his predecessor's footsteps and report on a monthly basis a series of key performance indicators designed to evaluate his department's performance. These metrics had been in place for years in the company and had become a standard and accepted way of reporting operational performance. Measurements included things like total revenue, total cost of sales, total inventory dollars and turns, performance to customer request dates, and departmental cost versus budget comparisons.

In order to produce this information, two or three members of Reginald's team spent a minimum of one week and often closer to two weeks of dedicated time each month manually gathering and analyzing the data and calculating final numbers on which to report. In addition to his team's efforts, Reginald personally spent one to two full days each month preparing the slides for the executive and customer meetings. Needless to say, there was a significant amount of effort and resources expended producing this information every month—but despite all the work that was going into them, Reginald had a nagging feeling that the numbers they were collecting were too high-level and did not properly represent the true performance of his team or their key operational processes. He didn't feel comfortable trying to make significant changes so early in his new job, however, so he kept quiet about his doubts.

After about six months in his role, Reginald was frustrated with the time-consuming and cumbersome routine of producing and delivering these measurements for executives and customers. There were many months when the team's efforts went entirely unnoticed because the executives' and customers' schedules were too full to even have a review meeting—and in the few months when the review sessions were held, Reginald was grilled by the audience with the same detailed and in-depth questions about what each measurement represented, how the information was gathered and calculated, and how the results could be improved. It seemed to him that no matter what data was reported, it was never understood or appreciated by his audience, and he left each meeting angry and agitated. He finally realized that he needed to drive a change in the existing reporting and metrics if he wanted to make the sessions and information more effective.

The first step in making a positive change was gathering input from key team leaders responsible for running the day-to-day operations. Over the course of several conference calls, Reginald asked each leader to review his or her key activities and current performance goals to determine which areas he or she felt could benefit from performance measurement. He encouraged the leaders to create numbers and reports that 1) were meaningful to the customers; 2) could predict in some way when the process was delivering less than expected; 3) were simple to understand and intuitive to the executive and customer audience; and 4) were easy to calculate and create on a monthly basis.

After a few weeks of brainstorming and creating, Reginald's team presented him with a recommendation. The leaders felt that in order to meet everyone's needs and all of Reginald's criteria, producing a weekly scorecard would be the best solution. The proposed scorecard had seven key measurements: number of orders processed within four hours; number of orders entered without manual intervention; number of customer orders on hold, and the reason for the hold; number of orders on backlog; revenue of backlogged orders; number of products causing backorders; and total revenue versus expected revenue. Each number to be reported was given a target and a range that represented whether the team's performance was green (on track), yellow (slightly off track), or red (needed improvement).

Reginald was excited about his team's ideas, and he worked with the IT team to create an automated group of reports that could be easily and quickly entered into the team's scorecard. Then, in order to test the new system's effectiveness and ease of use, Reginald held a weekly session with his team to review the results. What he discovered at these meetings was that this new method of reporting gave him some added bonuses in leading the operations: the scorecard allowed him to monitor how his team was performing on a weekly basis and to quickly make changes to improve a process before a major disaster hit. In addition, the data in the scorecard gave his team advance warning of any potential train wrecks in the business, which minimized the panic and interruptions that had frequently occurred under the old system, and because the fields were so precise and easy to measure, it cut way down on the time Reginald and his team had to spend accumulating and organizing data.

Reginald replaced the old reporting with this new scorecard in his review sessions with customers and the executives, and they all loved the new format and found the information meaningful and easy to understand. And because Reginald was using this same information to lead his team every week, he was no longer frustrated with producing reports and information no one looked at when a review session was missed. Reginald's ingenuity not only freed up his team's time to perform meaningful work, it also gave his team an opportunity to continuously improve its performance.

People Leadership Action Steps to Measuring with Purpose

1. Think about what measurements or reports your team currently produces. How can they be adjusted to be more purpose-driven?

2. Have you ever been part of a team or company that effectively used metrics? Think about what kind of impact it made on your organization.

"What's measured improves."

—Peter F. Drucker

20
Celebrate Successes

Often in business and in life, we get so focused on achieving goals and executing day-to-day activities that we forget to celebrate our successes—or we only celebrate completion of those tasks or projects we consider significant in scale. And yet scholars in behavioral science have proven over and over again that one of the best ways to get individuals to be more productive is praise them in some way for *all* of their accomplishments, regardless of the size. In order to maintain forward progress, it's important to acknowledge even the smallest tasks.

Celebrating success is one of the areas in which I get the most pushback from managers when I work with them on leading their teams. "We need to stay focused on work; we don't have time to celebrate," they tell me. Or they ask, "Why do I need to praise them? I don't need praise to get things done." Or they express my personal favorite: "Workers these days got coddled too much by their parents; I don't have time to babysit them and tell them they did a good job." When I hear these statements, I remind the executives that, like it or not, most human beings enjoy a good celebration. In fact, many of us will work twice as hard when we know there is a prize of some sort at the end of the journey. I tell all the leaders I work with to try celebrating success with their teams and see what results they can achieve in doing so.

Celebrating success as a people leader means:

- Being in tune with your team's actions.
- Creating meaningful rewards.
- Being consistent about offering recognition.

Stay in tune with your team's actions.

Most people leaders are expected to play a dual role: they are expected to manage their own set of activities and goals and also those of their team. This set of responsibilities can cause even the strongest leaders to lose sight of what is happening within their teams. Work days can fly by in what seems like an instant, making it very easy to become disconnected from the day-to-day actions of your employees—and when you are not in tune with your people's efforts, you cannot celebrate their accomplishments.

Difficult as it may feel, it is essential to remain connected and in tune with your team in some shape or form. You can check in with them by holding regular staff meetings, requesting frequent written updates, or even conducting a quick daily call to review key actions for the day. One of the keys behind these progress reviews is to share successes. Ask your team what they have completed or what they feel most proud of having done lately. If you are reviewing a particular project, record any major milestones that have been completed.

As your team members talk, listen and take note of what they are sharing. You will find that some individuals express pride and joy in doing things that may appear to be small tasks to you but feel like massive wins for them. For instance, maybe the person finally made a phone call to that one prospect he has been avoiding for weeks. Sure, at first brush this appears like a simple phone call; for the employee, however, making this call was like slaying a giant. The key for you as the leader is to be aware of what is exciting and important to each individual person and to commend him or her for executing those tasks.

The magnitude of the feat at hand may be a good indicator of what type of celebration is appropriate—but remember, all achievements require celebration of some sort. When you're handing out "high fives," be sure to recognize every individual's successes. High performers often get all of the attention while their less-visible peers are rolling their eyes, making snide comments, and feeling less motivated to achieve anything going forward. Don't let this happen with your team; keep in mind that celebrations are most effective when they are shared with everyone, not just your brightest stars!

Create meaningful rewards.

Acknowledging successes on your team does not have to be a huge time consumer, and it doesn't have to be expensive. There are literally hundreds of ways to reward your team members' work with meaningful tokens of appreciation—all it takes is a little bit of time and creativity.

One of the easiest and most often overlooked ways of rewarding your employees is a simple, heartfelt verbal thank-you. Your delivery, however, must be authentic. If you do not really appreciate the work, don't thank your team member for it. People are smarter than most managers give them credit for, and they can smell a fake expression of gratitude from a mile away.

A handwritten note of appreciation for a job well done is also a great way to appreciate your team members' efforts. You will be surprised at the reaction from people, even those reared during the electronic age, when they receive a physical note thanking them for their efforts.

Food is another great token of appreciation. It never ceases to amaze me what a simple snack can do to make an individual feel acknowledged. We must all be programmed with some fond memory of having snack time at school, because even as adults, we love to be rewarded with food. Surprising your team with celebratory snacks during the day can be fun and effective, especially when you give them a few minutes off to enjoy them. And lunch—well, that's a big hit with most teams! Who doesn't appreciate a free lunch? Giving spa certificates, movie passes, or sports tickets are also simple, fairly inexpensive ways to say "Great job and thanks."

One of my favorite forms of celebrating success is to give a person time off for a job well done. When I was a manager, I would often surprise my team by coming in on a Friday afternoon and saying, "Hey, you have all done such amazing things this week, I want you to go ahead and leave—go spend time with your family!" The trick then, of course, was to actually make them leave and go enjoy their free time.

The celebratory technique that I have found works better than material rewards, surprisingly enough, is a simple one: public recognition of an individual's accomplishments in front of his or her peers and other leaders. Most people love for others to know they did a great job, and recognizing them publicly makes them feel good in a way that even a trip to a spa can't.

No matter what you decide to do, just make sure you don't forget to find creative ways to celebrate with your team; when you do celebrate, you'll see their overall performance skyrocket.

Celebrate consistently.

Just like anything in life, in order to maintain the benefits of celebrating successes, you must do it in moderation—but you must also do it consistently. Organizations that only celebrate the big stuff can create a discouraging work environment for their employees; if people believe their hard work will only be appreciated when they reach huge milestones, they will slack off or perform at the lowest possible level they can while still keeping their jobs. Departments that rarely or never provide any sort of recognition of their employees for a job well done are filled with individuals who feel underappreciated.

In order to generate consistent positive action and momentum on their teams, people leaders must celebrate successes on a regular basis. If your attitude is that your employees' reward is their paycheck and they should be happy just to have jobs, you can rest assured that—at best—your team will do just what you are rewarding them to do: work for their paychecks. If you celebrate every action, on the other hand, the meaning behind the recognition is lost. For instance, I worked with one leader who was really good about bringing in lunch every month for her team as a means of recognizing their hard work. At first, celebrating with the team in this way improved productivity and performance; over time, however, the team began to *expect* the lunch, and their boss's well-intended gesture lost its power to motivate.

Celebrating successes, then, must be done consistently but with moderation in order to deliver effective, profitable results. I've found it's most effective to celebrate with a mix of big and small celebrations that are peppered throughout the year. Whatever approach to expressing gratitude for your team you choose to implement, remain diligent in showing your team members how much you appreciate their work, and your organization will be rewarded with productivity ten times greater than you can imagine.

Celebrating Success in Action

As the leader of a large distribution center, Cain oversaw more than two hundred people. His team was responsible for all activities associated with receiving product, managing inventory, and shipping customer orders for one of the fastest-growing divisions in the company. Cain had been at the facility for over five years, and for the past four years, the team had consistently met every performance measurement goal that was created for them. However, as the division the warehouse operation supported continued its significant growth spurt, the expectations on Cain's team's overall performance increased accordingly. This meant that in his fifth year there, the daily outputs of orders his team was expected to complete increased to one and half times what had previously been expected—without hiring new employees.

When Cain found out what the new expectations for his team were, he was emotionally torn: he knew that these were exciting times for the company—the growth in revenue was unprecedented, and the future looked extremely bright—but he also knew that his team was the last and most forgotten piece of the delivery support network, and that they were being asked to perform a miracle. People on his team had already been complaining that they felt underappreciated and were tired of working so hard with no recognition; now he was going to have to tell them that they were expected to do a lot more with the same amount of resources. He wasn't sure what to do, but he knew something had to be done to reignite his team—and quickly.

Fortunately, Cain's department had an employee activity committee that was responsible for representing their peers and coming up with fun activities for the team throughout the year. Cain knew they would be the best group of individuals to help him through this potentially painful dilemma, so he went to them and explained the predicament. The team wasn't happy about what they were hearing at first; they knew their teammates already felt like the forgotten and unloved stepchild in the company, and they knew that this news would only make things worse. But when Cain asked them to turn the challenge into a means of proving the warehouse operations department's value to the rest of the company, they decided to find a way to ignite their coworkers' passion.

One of the first things Cain's employee activity committee recommended was for Cain to recognize all his employees for the jobs they were already performing. The team felt that no one in the company appreciated their efforts, they told him, so doing something to let them know the company did notice would go a long way in making them feel better about their jobs.

The committee threw out a few ideas and finally came to the conclusion that one of their coworkers' favorite things to do was eat, so if Cain wanted to express gratitude for his group's hard work, food was a great place to start.

Cain loved the idea and ran it by his director for approval. Having received the go-ahead, Cain announced to the employee population that they were going to be treated to lunch for their hard work over the past year. When he asked the employee committee about the reaction to the lunch from their coworkers, they told him they received comments like "It's about time someone appreciated us" and "That's awesome, I am glad someone finally noticed us."

Encouraged by his team's initial reaction, Cain decided to take the celebration one step further by making the lunch a catered buffet and enlisting his management team to serve the food to the employees themselves. As each person came through the line, Cain and his managers looked each person in the eye and said, "Thank you for your hard work this last year." They were gratified to find that their thank-yous were met with big, confident smiles and a lot of statements like "You are very welcome, just doing my job."

The lunch was a big hit. For the next few weeks, the warehouse operation was buzzing with activity—the workers were excited and energized because they felt they were appreciated. Now, however, it was time for Cain to share the news of the upcoming increased volume expectations with his team. Before he did, he consulted with the employee committee once again to get their thoughts on how to best communicate this news. They told Cain that they believed the team would be excited to hear about the company's growth because they were still high from the celebration lunch and thrilled that the rest of the organization knew they even existed, but that Cain should continue the success recognition by sprinkling in cookie breaks or ice cream parties when certain small milestones were accomplished. Cain thanked the team for their input and assured them that he would implement their suggestions more consistently throughout the year.

The next day, Cain told his team about the division's growth and the corresponding increased volume expectations—and as the committee had said they would be, they team was excited by the news. A few employees even remarked that they were ready for the challenge and that they would show the company they could do it. Relieved, Cain encouraged his team to simply do their best.

As time progressed and the volume increased, the warehouse staff did an amazing job keeping up with the increased expectations and growth. On a periodic basis, Cain brought in cookies, ice cream, or lunch for the team to celebrate their continued success, and he and his management team also made an authentic effort to regularly walk through the warehouse and thank employees personally for their hard work and dedication.

By listening to his employees and rewarding them for their efforts in a way that worked for them, Cain made his team more productive and effective—and a lot happier.

People Leadership Action Steps to Celebrating Successes

1. Think about how you currently celebrate your team's successes. Are your methods appreciated by your team?

2. Come up with some creative, cost-effective ways you can celebrate with your team.

3. Reflect on a time when your successes were rewarded in a meaningful way. What was done for you and/or the team? How did it impact future performance?

"Celebrate what you want to see more of."

—Tom Peters

21

Influence Chicken Little

In the oft-told folk tale Henny Penny, most commonly known as Chicken Little in the United States, a young chick is hit on the head by a falling acorn and believes it's a sign that the world is coming to an end. In an effort to warn his town of the impending doom, the young chicken runs through the streets frantically yelling, "The sky is falling, the sky is falling!" This phrase, "The sky is falling," has become commonplace in business and in life and means that disaster is imminent—and as you lead people, you will most likely encounter Chicken Little personalities somewhere along your journey.

Chicken Littles are easy to spot—they're the ones who are anxious and concerned and who appear to resist or find fault in most everything, especially new decisions and requests to change. In an effort to prevent them from creating a disaster where one needn't exist in your organization, it is critical to influence the Chicken Littles in your team.

Influencing Chicken Littles requires:

- Being aware of and understanding their world.
- Providing them with an alternative view of the situation.
- Engaging them in a positive "go forward" plan.

Understand their world.

Chicken Littles are anxious personalities who are typically outspoken and oftentimes a little dramatic. Their nervous energy and fears can quickly mesmerize and inspire large groups of individuals to join them in their anxious states. In short, if Chicken Littles are left to their own devices, they can convince anyone in your organization that the "sky is falling."

The first key to influencing this less-than-positive behavior is to simply be aware when you have a Chicken Little in your organization. As a people leader, you can easily spot their nervous energy by listening to their comments about their daily activities or responsibilities. Chicken Littles tend to see the world as scary and negative. You will hear them say things like "I am worried that . . ." or "That will never work here" or "That decision is going to cause a major disaster for everyone." When you hear phrases like these, do not ignore them or brush them off; unlikely as it may seem, sentiments like these can quickly permeate the rest of your team. Chicken Littles need to be addressed directly.

One of the best ways to defuse a Chicken Little personality is simply to listen. Let the team member rant and rave and spill his or her guts to you about his or her concern. What you will most likely find is that his or her fear of loss, fear of pain, or fear of outcome is running higher than that of the other members of your team. The more you listen to the Chicken Little, the more you will find that he or she is "scared to death" of something that may seem trivial to you. By listening and asking questions, you can better understand the reasons behind his or her fears and uncertainties. Once you recognize what is driving the Chicken Little's anxious energy and concern, you will be better equipped to influence his or her behaviors.

Provide an alternative view.

Remember that Chicken Littles see life through very dark glasses. These personality types tend to take every perceived problem and make them into very large mountains, regardless of their real size. To these individuals, nothing about life or work looks rosy at all; therefore, they can greatly benefit from seeing an alternate view of their world.

You can influence a Chicken Little's behavior simply by taking the time to discuss and brainstorm alternate views of reality with him or her. For instance, when a Chicken Little team member hears that your company sales numbers have decreased slightly since last month, he or she may immediately fret about the impending demise of the company—a worry that stems from the fear that he or she will lose his or her job. It's important, then, that the team member get pertinent facts about the situation.

Maybe sales patterns are always down in this particular month of the year, or maybe sales are down this month because customers are waiting for a new product that's coming next month. As a people leader, it is your responsibility to help the Chicken Little see beyond his or her negative view of the world.

In your discussions with the Chicken Littles of your team, you may find that no matter what view you present, they will still be anxious and concerned; if that is the case, keep digging into the facts. You may uncover some valid concerns that need to be addressed. Do not let them only be the bearers of bad news; instead, ask them to participate in making the situation better by coming up with potential solutions. Interrupt their anxious nature by saying things like "Thank you for sharing that concern with me. I was not aware of the gravity of the situation. I would really like your input into how we can fix it." Don't be surprised when the Chicken Little responds with, "Well, it's not really that big of a deal. I think there's a simple way to make it better for everyone." Oftentimes it just takes offering the Chicken Littles an alternative view of their worlds to draw them out of their agitated and fearful states.

Engage in a positive "go forward" plan.

By acknowledging the Chicken Littles on your team, understanding their worlds, and helping them see different sides of the situation, you are priming them to move into a state of forward progress instead of fearful decline. The next step is to try to help them see life differently on their own, without your intervention.

If you want your Chicken Littles to start thinking before they react anxiously, it is helpful to subtly establish a positive "go forward" plan that will allow them to control their negative behavior. In other words, because these are anxious types to begin with, you can't just say, "Hey quit being so anxious and start being rational"; instead, you need to help them create a simple routine that they can follow whenever they start to spiral. A Chicken Little improvement plan could be as easy as 1, 2, 3. You might ask your Chicken Littles to talk themselves through these steps: 1) I quietly acknowledge that I am feeling anxious, and I reflect upon why in order to get to the root of my concern; 2) I research the facts and look for the positive alternative to each of my concerns; 3) I offer solutions to make the situation better and share them with my team members. The key is finding a plan that works for the individual to help him or her break his or her habitual pattern of being the town crier.

Change in any situation or of any behavior generally takes at least twenty-one days, and as a people leader, it is your responsibility to support Chicken Littles in their growth plans. Work with them through this transition to keep them focused on letting go of this anxious behavior, and encourage them to keep moving forward. You will be pleasantly surprised when you see their Chicken Little traits begin to fade away—and when they begin to stop their unproductive and destructive behavior before it spreads through your entire organization.

Influencing Chicken Little in Action

Helena, a member of the customer service team, was a self-proclaimed nervous wreck. In the workplace, this anxiety manifested itself every time Helena encountered a problem, no matter how small, or whenever something new was introduced to the organization. And when she got concerned about something, she openly expressed her fears and worries with anyone who would listen, using exaggerated phrases like "worst ever," "major disaster," and "biggest nightmare ever" to describe her perception of the situation—whether she was talking to executives, peers, or customers.

Helena presented quite a conundrum to her manager, Casey, who was the director of the customer service team. On the one hand, she drove him crazy because, according to her, the sky was always falling. There were days when her nervous energy made him wish she were part of another organization. On the other hand, Helena's knowledge of and expertise with customer orders made her a critical resource within his department.

Helena was responsible for managing what were referred to as "problem orders"—orders for custom and complex telecommunication systems that were to be installed in large businesses and enterprises. Because each of these orders was specific to a particular customer's needs and a particular installation location, the configuration and product rules were customized for each customer site. In an attempt to make the order process flow more smoothly, the company had put systems in place that automatically compared and validated the customer order details to those of the custom configuration quote. In the event the system encountered any mismatch between the order and the quote, the orders were automatically placed on a system hold and labeled "problem orders"—and the only way to remove that hold was to correct the issue, which required an employee with in-depth knowledge of the product configuration requirements.

Because Helena had originally worked in the quotation tool team, she understood the product requirements and validation rules, which made her the best person to deal with these problem orders; however, she was causing too much disruption with the customers and the entire order management organization because of her Chicken Little behavior. Something had to change.

Casey decided he needed to somehow influence Helena's behavior before she caused further chaos in the organization. The next time she approached him with a frantic concern, instead of reacting immediately to provide a solution, he asked Helena to give him a bit more context for her doomsday view of the issue at hand. As she expressed fear after fear about the issue, Casey recognized two things: 1) Some of her facts were misinterpretations of reality; and 2) The real root of Helena's anxiety was her fear of losing her job for ineffective performance.

Once Casey understood what was going on in Helena's world, he was equipped to offer her a different point of view. He let her express her con-cerns for about twenty minutes, and then he began to offer clarifications of the issues Helena had brought up. As he did so, Helena was surprised and relieved to find out that some of her information had been inaccurate.

Once Helena had all the up-to-date facts, Casey began to address her personal fears about her job performance by asking her how many times she had encountered an issue that she could not resolve. Her first response was, "All the time, I have tons of examples"—but Casey kept a close eye on how long orders on hold remained on hold, and he knew this couldn't be the case. The numbers demonstrated that Helena resolved almost every issue within one day or less. There were a few exceptions—some issues that took two or more days to resolve—but they were just that: exceptions. As Casey showed her that she was really doing a stellar job and often exceeding expectations, Helena's nervous energy dissipated. She acknowledged that she had overreacted and expressed again that she had a tendency to worry.

Casey knew that Helena needed to somehow break her worry cycle at work because her Chicken Little behavior was going to be damaging for the company in the long term. So, before they finished their conversation, he suggested to Helena that the next time she got worried, she try to stop herself from telling the world and focus instead on gathering the facts and looking at her concerns from different vantage points. When she couldn't work through her worries on her own, he asked her to call him to talk through them rather than sharing them with the team.

Helena agreed to Casey's proposal, and over the course of a month, he received at least one phone call a day from Helena about different issues. Each time, he walked Helena through the agreed-upon process of focusing on the facts and looking at alternate views, and by the end of the month, her Chicken Little behavior had practically disappeared. She stopped driving Casey, his team, and herself crazy with worry, and her productivity increased by 50 percent. It took some time, but in the end, Casey's persistence in influencing Helena's Chicken Little behavior paid off.

People Leadership Action Steps to Influencing Chicken Little

1. Think about whether you have any Chicken Littles on your team. How do you know?

2. Come up with some steps can you take to influence the Chicken Littles on your team.

3. Think of a leader you've had who demonstrated good Chicken Little management. What did he or she do that was most effective?

"People who let events and circumstances dictate their lives are living reactively. That means that they don't act on life, they only react to it."

—Stedman Graham

22
Improve Leadership Continuously

M any businesses and organizations expend vast resources on continuous process improvement. These are considered quality practices and are designed to ensure that a company's processes, products, and services are effective, efficient, and flexible enough to meet the ever-changing needs of their business and customers. When it comes to people leadership, however, companies rarely invest the resources to improve the quality of the frontline executives, managers, or supervisors. Simply put, no resources are expended on people and leadership skills—but they should be. Just like processes, products, and services, people leaders need to be continuously refined and improved.

Continuously improving your leadership skills requires:
- Focusing on personal growth.
- Being open and flexible to change.
- Finding a mentor or coach.

Focus on growing.

With all the demands placed on you each day, it's easy to overlook the importance of evolving your personal leadership skills and knowledge. There may even be times in your career when you might believe you have hit the pinnacle in the executive rank and think you have nothing further to develop. My personal experience, however, has taught me that the moment you stop caring about personal growth is the moment your leadership effectiveness starts to die a slow death. People leadership requires constant personal growth. After all, how can you encourage others to grow and improve if you don't expect it of and experience it for yourself?

Twenty years ago, you had to attend a seminar to learn about leadership, but now your choices also include reading a self-improvement or business book, watching a TED Talk, watching a personal-growth expert on YouTube, finding an app on your smartphone, or listening to a podcast, among other opportunities. Personally, I love to read, so I have pored over hundreds of personal-growth, change, and self-improvement books. Many of them were about the topic of leadership; however, most of them were focused on how to make me a more motivated, balanced, well-rounded, and successful person. Growing personally does not have to be "all business." It can also include things like mastering a new hobby or playing a new sport. The key is that you do something that will keep you progressing forward and not getting stale in your life.

About ten years into my career, I discovered that my ability to lead people successfully had a direct correlation with my personal state of being. What I mean by this is that every time I slacked on personal development, I was less effective, more stressed, and imbalanced in my work efforts, and so—surprise!—was my team. I realized that my personal growth had a huge impact on my team's results. That's why people leaders must be willing to learn and put into practice something new for themselves every day. Psychologists have discovered that learning a new hobby or skill makes us feel alive as individuals and in turn makes us more effective in the things we choose to do. And learning does not have to be boring, hard, or time-consuming; dedicate just fifteen minutes a day to learning something new and positive for you, and you and your team will thrive.

Be open and flexible to change.

In order to improve anything, change must happen. Most of us think we abhor change of any kind, and yet each of us changes every day, whether we think we do or not. One of my least favorite beliefs is that people can't change. This belief is absurd; of course people can change! Dr. Suess's popular holiday story *How the Grinch Stole Christmas*, in which the Grinch goes from being a nasty, mean, heartless, stealing Santa Claus impostor to being a happy, kind, loving, and generous person, is a perfect testimony to the fact that even the nastiest of people can change—if they want to. And just like the Grinch, every one of us can improve our situation if we truly have the desire to change.

The real problem is not that people *can't* change—it's that most people *won't* change. We trick ourselves into believing that wherever we are in life is where we are supposed to be, and we get comfortable with and secure in our current surroundings, whether or not we actually feel satisfied. The unknown seems far too scary, so we make no effort to do something different. This fear translates into an unwillingness to be open to new ways of being or doing things—but it is this lack of motivation to change that keeps us from reaching most of our deepest desires.

If you want to be effective as a people leader, it is essential that you be open and flexible to change. This requires you to be interested and excited to discover, learn, and try new and different ways of operating. When you listen to that TED Talk or watch your favorite motivation teacher online, be open to trying out the techniques the speaker suggests. As you are reading this book about becoming a better people leader, be open to using some of the ideas outlined with your team.

As I mentioned in the last chapter, it normally takes twenty-one days to make a positive change in your (or someone else's) life. Change starts with being open and willing and taking that first step. I encourage you to become more change-friendly, not only because it will help you but also because as your team sees you transform and improve, they will take steps to do so as well.

Get a mentor or coach.

Businesses invest millions of dollars on professional staff or outside consultants to improve their costs, processes, and systems—and yet when it comes to improving leaders, many companies only hire executive coaches for their CEOs and vice presidents. I think that anyone who directs or leads people should have a mentor or coach. Leadership coaches are like personal trainers: they teach us new training techniques, push us beyond our innate laziness and our limiting beliefs, and keep us moving toward our goals. Effective people leadership requires constant learning and growth—and that's a lot easier when you have someone to guide you and give you consistent support as you evolve.

Good coaches and mentors strategize with you on what actions to take when people challenges come up, and they provide you with new ways to inspire and motivate your team. More important, a good mentor is a sounding board for you—someone who will listen to your challenges as a people leader and help you feel like you're not doing it all on your own.

People leadership is not learned overnight; it's a journey. Focusing on continuous leadership improvement allows you to successfully meet your organization's ever-changing needs.

Continuously Improve Leadership in Action

Dana was the newest and youngest member of the newly formed operations team for Nortel's new product line. Her boss, Walter, had hired her because he was impressed with her resume and because she was clearly ambitious and motivated to succeed. He knew Dana was going to progress through the leadership ranks quickly.

Dana was initially hired to administer all new customer contracts that were being negotiated for purchasing the new products. Equipped with her "I can do anything" attitude, Dana quickly mastered various roles and projects in Walter's organization. No matter the type or size of the challenge given to her, Dana always found a way to get the job done quickly and effectively. She was swiftly making a name for herself in the company; leaders from other departments were taking notice and were frequently asking Walter if Dana could help their teams implement strategic objectives and projects because her results were so good.

Walter recognized that Dana was a strong asset to his team, and he wanted to make sure he did everything he needed to support her continued growth and success—so, since she had never supervised a team before, and because she had told him in her interview and in conversations since then that she loved to learn, he decided to send her to some leadership and motivational seminars. Dana learned a number of new techniques at these events, and each time she came back from one, she was more personally motivated and driven than before.

After Dana had attended a number of these seminars, Walter felt comfortable assigning her to her first managerial role and allowing her to hire a team to support her with the contracts process. As expected, Dana mastered working with people and leading teams very quickly. The individuals on her team were superstars, and they loved working with her.

Because of her leadership success and continued ability to get results in anything she was assigned, Dana was quickly promoted through the executive ranks. Over the course of three years, she moved from manager to senior manager to director of various organizations, and with each new team, the results were the same: a stellar performance. Dana continued to exceed Walter's expectations as she grew into each role, and he was convinced that she had no limits when it came to achieving the objectives and challenges presented to her. He continued to invest in Dana's personal growth and learning, and he even dedicated his own personal time to providing her mentorship and offering her insight into his own leadership tactics.

About five years after she first came to work for him, Walter noticed that something was beginning to change in Dana. Her positive attitude and zest to improve, personally and professionally, had all but disappeared, and her team's results were slowly starting to decline. Out of concern for her, Walter engaged her in a very open and candid conversation about the results he was seeing. In the past, when they had held similar discussions, Dana had always been open to feedback and input on how to improve. This time, however, she was stiff, had her arms crossed, and appeared very agitated— and as Walter disclosed his concerns, she offered up lots of complaints and excuses. She blamed her inability to perform on the continued cost-cutting, headcount reductions, and the overall executive edict to "do more with less." In a nutshell, she told Walter that executive leadership was the cause of all the problems and that she had no control over what was happening.

It was clear to Walter that Dana had fallen victim to the "it's not my fault" attitude that many of his other leaders lived by on a daily basis. He reminded her that she actually had more resources in the current environment than she'd had in years and that her previous performance exceeded expectations. This comment only made Dana even more frustrated—and that's when Walter recognized that this was not the same Dana he'd worked with for the past five years. Something was going on, and he needed to get to the bottom of it.

Walter switched gears and asked Dana how things were going in her personal life. She shared that she was having a tough time: she was having relationship problems, and she was so stressed out at work that she was letting her health and fitness programs falter. Walter continued to listen to Dana, and at the end of their conversation, he encouraged her to take some time to think about what she could do to make her personal and professional life better. He assured her that she was important to the company and that he wanted to help her improve. Although she was obviously frustrated by his request, Dana promised Walter that she would think about it and get back to him.

Over the next few weeks, Dana couldn't let the conversation with Walter go. It was really bugging her. How in the heck was she supposed to know what was going on? But as she reflected on what had changed in the past few years, she had an aha moment—she realized she had stopped growing. She had gotten so caught up in climbing the career ladder that she'd forgotten that what had enabled her to excel and lead her teams was her zest for learning and improving. When she had this realization, she was actually excited to go back to Walter to share it with him.

Walter was relieved when Dana told him what the problem was, and he pushed and supported Dana to work on improving herself. She started reading again, attended a few new seminars, and began her mentoring sessions again with Walter—and over the course of a few months, her personal life and her work performance began to change for the better. In focusing on continuously improving herself, Dana made herself—and her team—far more productive.

People Leadership Action Steps to Continuously Improve Leadership

1. Think about how you continuously improve your people leadership. What have you done lately?

2. Come up with some actions you can take to improve your leadership style. What resources do you need to make those actions happen?

3. Think about a leader you know who focuses on constant improvement and a well-rounded lifestyle. What qualities do you admire most in him or her? Can you emulate any of his or her actions?

"Leadership development is a lifetime journey, not a quick trip."

—John Maxwell

23
Empower People

I've heard over a hundred business executives say, "We tried empowering people in our company, and it failed. We just need to tell people what to do." Wrong. Leaders are responsible for whether or not empowerment works. I have worked in and with both organizations that were successful in empowering their people and organizations that failed, and I've learned that there's a technique and an art behind it. Over the years, empowerment has been misinterpreted and implemented as simply allowing individuals to make decisions on their own, without their bosses' or managers' approval. But that's not what it is. Empowerment is a process that requires more than just handing your employees the keys to the kingdom and saying, "You're in charge now—good luck!"

Empowering people requires certain mechanics and techniques, including:
- Fostering a proper mindset for both the leader and the employee.
- Setting boundaries and expectations.
- Coaching along the way.

Foster an empowerment mindset.
Empowerment is a two-way street: both leaders and their employees must be willing to be part of the process. It starts with leaders trusting, accepting, and appreciating the strengths, diversity, and character that each

"empoweree" brings to the team. Leaders who attempt to empower people without an open and trusting mindset will always fail to empower their teams because they will always be second-guessing their employees' effectiveness. Any time that kind of doubt is present, the only thing that gets created is frustration for everyone involved.

Just as important as the leader having a trusting mindset is the team members having an empowered mindset. They must be open and amenable to evaluating opportunities and making decisions. In any organization, there is a mix of people who want to make decisions on their own and those who are quite content to do what they are told. People leaders must take the time to understand how receptive each of their employees is to acting as an "empoweree." If an individual is not open to taking control, do not push the concept on him or her. Your efforts will be better rewarded if you find those people who desire the challenge and opportunity for more authority.

A good way to ensure that both a leader and his or her employee have the mindset to be empowered is to ask a few simple questions of both of them: What does empowerment mean to you? How do you feel about taking on or letting go of decision-making authority? How does being empowered or allowing empowerment make you feel? The responses to these questions will provide good insight into whether a mutual empowerment mindset exists between the people leader and his or her team member.

Set boundaries and expectations.

Enabling others to make their own choices and decisions is much more effective when people leaders provide parameters within which their employees can operate. I like to call this concept giving your employees the "what" instead of the "how." As I previously stated, empowerment does not mean just handing over the keys to the kingdom and walking away. Nor does it mean doling out so many rules that your employees have no real chance to create their own solutions. Rules squash creativity and freedom; boundaries provide general guidelines and information that help your team members make effective choices. For instance, if you are empowering a customer service representative to make a customer happy, then reviewing any existing policies is a must. During this review, it is critical to express to your employees what latitude exists in playing inside or outside the boundaries of those guidelines. If the policy has to be followed to a T, then there is effectively no empowerment, because the person cannot deviate from the rules under any circumstance. On the other hand, if the employee can make any decision at all, with no regard to the impact to the business, there is too much empowerment.

Empowerment requires establishing boundaries and guidelines that can properly lead the "empoweree" to the most effective choice for all parties involved in the situation. In our customer service scenario, if the direction provided is simply, "If the customer is unhappy, do what it takes to make them happy," then the results might be detrimental to both the customer and the company. It would be more effective to instruct the employee to consider how the choices they provide to the customer impact all parties involved. Does the decision they want to make cost a lot of money to implement, or will it generate goodwill and increased revenue in the future? Will doing nothing for the customer cause lost revenue now and in the future? Remind team members to always think about whether the customer is being reasonable and, if not, what the ongoing cost of keeping a customer who is never satisfied might be.

Providing guidelines and parameters like these as considerations in the decision-making process empowers your employees to create more successful results for all parties involved.

Coach along the way.

When people hear the word *coach*, many think of professionals in the world of sports or self-mastery. However, one of the most important things you can be as a people leader is a coach for your employees. When you begin the practice of empowering people, consider that this may be the first time in their lives that they have been allowed to be autonomous and think on their own, not only in their professional lives, but also their personal lives. Some people may have been micromanaged by others—their parents, their partners—throughout life and have little to no experience in acting on their own. Other individuals may have encountered "horrible bosses" in their careers who never gave them the authority to decide anything for themselves. Regardless of their experience level with empowerment, coaching your employees throughout the process is essential.

Again, empowerment is not bestowing a title or a rank upon someone and leaving him or her on his or her own to survive and succeed. Your team members need your support and coaching along the way. There will be occasions when individuals may be at an impasse and unable to make a decision; when that happens, they need to know they can come to you for input and guidance. If and when you are asked for support, remember that your role is to listen and coach, not to solve the problem for them. Empowering leaders understand how important it is for their team members to formulate their own solutions as often as possible. This requires asking questions, encouraging brainstorming, offering your team members an objective point of view, and then trusting them to make the best decision possible.

Empowered teams have a proven track record of providing excellent service and high productivity.

Empowering People in Action

Scott was a new employee in Edith's process and projects organization. One of Edith's team's major projects for the year was a corporate initiative to outsource warehouse and distribution operations to an outside supplier. In order for this project to be successful, Edith knew she needed someone on her team who had experience in all aspects of the current warehouse and distribution center. She chose Scott from a pool of six other candidates because he had a proven track record with each major function in the current operation, including shipping, receiving, customer returns, and inventory management.

Scott had never participated in a project this big or strategic, but he was a dedicated employee who was well versed in the department's day-to-day processes and activities, and Edith was certain that he was the right person to work with the selected provider to build a warehouse facility and create operations processes that would meet the current best-in-class performance metrics and customer needs.

In their initial discussions about Scott's new role, Edith told Scott that her leadership style was very empowering. She expected each of her team members to make decisions about and own his or her piece of any project. She asked Scott if he was comfortable being responsible and accountable for the facility requirements she had outlined. He was a bit hesitant at first; he told Edith that he had never been given this much authority in his previous roles, that his former managers had always wanted to make all the decisions and maintain all the control. He said he wasn't afraid to make decisions; he just needed her assurance that he really would have the freedom to act on his own, as well as full support from her if he had any questions.

Edith assured Scott that he would have full autonomy on the project and that she would be available whenever he needed her input or suggestions. Then she gave him his first major task: create a set of requirements for the soon-to-be-built facility, as well as a description of the key operational functions and processes that would need to be managed there on an ongoing basis. This document would be used as a guideline for potential suppliers to quote the price of warehouse facility as well as the cost of managing the operational functions. She gave Scott a deadline and left him to do it.

Scott finished the requested document one week ahead of schedule, and Edith was very pleased with his thoroughness and attention to detail. They sent it out to three potential suppliers, and after about a month, the proposals began to come in. Scott's next key task was to review the proposals, offer Edith feedback on the pros and cons of each one, and give his recommendation for which supplier they should choose. After reviewing Scott's assessment of the quotes, Edith was impressed and pleased with his initiative and decision-making methodology. She shared his input and recommendations with the executive team, who were also impressed, and they awarded the contract to Scott's company of choice.

Now it was time to enter the implementation stage of the project. Once again, Edith assigned Scott to work with the supplier. She shared with Scott that this project was extremely important to the company's strategy for the year and was being closely watched by the executive team, and she told him that the project must meet a specific deadline, budget number, and ongoing performance level in order to be seen as a success. She assured Scott that he could make the decisions he deemed necessary to meet the project deliverables as long as he stayed within the budget, timeline, and performance-level expectations. Scott confidently proceeded with his implementation tasks. As he went forward, Edith checked in with him each week to ensure that he was equipped with everything he needed to be a success and to allow him to bring forward any concerns or issues he needed coaching on.

With Edith's help, Scott finished the project on time and met all of the expectations that had been established by the leadership team. During a project debrief with Edith, Scott thanked her for giving him the opportunity to work on such an important project and told her how happy he was to have a management team that trusted and empowered him to use his strengths to make a positive impact for the company. In the years that followed, Scott turned out to be a dedicated and productive employee for the company.

People Leadership Action Steps to Empowering People

1. Think about what you currently do to empower your team members.

2. Come up with some steps you can take to empower them more.

3. Reflect upon a time when you have been both empowered and supported to make decisions or reach an important goal. What process was used to enable you to be successful?

"As we look ahead into the next century, leaders will be those who empower others."

—Bill Gates

24

Be Accessible

One of my adjunct professors in business graduate school was CEO of a major healthcare corporation. During one of our classes, he described his actions on his first day with the company: Upon assessing the elaborate furnishings in the office assigned to him, he immediately called the facilities staff to come to his office to make a few changes. When the facilities manager arrived at the office, the CEO requested that he remove of all the fancy furniture and fixtures and replace them with standard office furnishings that were simple, useful, and comparable to what the rest of the employee population used. He wanted to show the people in his company that he was accessible and was no more important than any member of his team just because he had the title of CEO, he told us—and he didn't want the fancy trappings of the executive suite to intimidate people from interacting with him. He also had the facilities staff remove his office door; his personality bordered on being introverted, he said, and the act of removing the door both demonstrated an open-door policy to his team and prevented him from closing himself off from the staff.

My fellow MBA students and I were amazed. Hearing this CEO of a Fortune 500 company describe his genuine desire to be accessible, as well as his tendency to be shy, was unfathomable to any of us; our image of corporate CEOs were people who expected ornate offices in ivory towers, enjoyed their status as top dog, and rarely interacted with anyone in their organization below the executive ranks. In short, this was one of the first CEOs we had encountered who felt that being accessible was important. His lesson about accessibility stuck with me long after I graduated from my program and began my own leadership journey.

Effective people leadership requires being accessible to people. You can't lead people without being available to them. And being accessible is not just about having an open-door policy—it means being friendly, easy to talk to, approachable, and reachable. But when I work with companies to help them improve their effectiveness, I frequently find CEOs, supervisors, and managers who are completely unavailable to their team, both physically and emotionally. These leaders often claim they don't have time to be bothered by their team members' problems or questions because their focus is on running the business; they believe that being accessible to their team members is a waste of their valuable time and is not essential to their overall business strategy. I have found, however, that being inaccessible to people is hugely detrimental to a team's effectiveness, because teams tend to mirror the qualities of their leaders: if a leader displays unapproachable behaviors, their team members will do the same, with their peers and even with their customers.

As people leaders, being accessible is critical, and it simply requires:

- Being present.
- Operating with an open mind and heart.
- Interacting with people on all levels of the organization.

Be present.

Being fully present when interacting with others is a key success factor in being an accessible people leader. Now more than ever, however, we are bombarded with multiple sources of input and demands, many of them seemingly coming at us at the same time, and it makes living in the so-called "now" feel virtually impossible.

I frequently hear people say that they don't have the luxury to live in the present because they are too overwhelmed with what needs to be done. When I ask questions and probe a little deeper into the source of this sense of overwhelm, I tend to uncover two main culprits: 1) demands on employees' time and energy for future decisions, goals, or events they're working toward; or 2) requests from executives or customers to explain and go over the details of things that have already transpired. In other words, all of the "noise" in their world is either future- or past-focused. It's just how we are conditioned to operate.

Here's the conundrum: the only activity we can actually control or impact is that which happens in the present moment. Think about it. We cannot genuinely affect the past (it's already done) or the future (it has yet to happen). And yet I would venture to guess that 95 percent of all interpersonal interactions take place while we are focused on the past or the future—in other words, while we are distracted. And distracted people are neither approachable nor accessible, even if they have a "my door is always open" or "I am always here for you" attitude.

In order to be approachable, people need to know you are interested in them *while* you are interacting with them. This means that when you are speaking with them in person, you make direct eye contact and resist the urge to shift your focus onto something or someone else. It also means that when you are in a conversation with a team member on the phone, you listen to what they are telling you instead of multitasking. Being fully present to someone in the moment you are with them makes them feel cared for and appreciated, and it makes them see you as friendly, trustworthy, and respectful.

It may sound nearly impossible to focus on the present, but all you have to do is think up some simple trigger or reminder to bring your attention the now. A few of my favorite techniques when I get distracted are to take a deep breath or to feel the pulse on my wrist. Those simple actions remind me that it is the present that counts. After all, if my heart and my breath weren't working *right now*, I would be dead. Give yourself some time to get centered and focused when interacting with your team members. If you need a moment to complete a thought or activity in order to do that, tell them you need a few minutes and finish what you're doing. Then tune into the "now," and give your team full access to your time and attention in the present moment.

Operate with an open mind and heart.

Being approachable also means keeping your heart and mind open to others' ideas and ways of being. This requires shifting your focus away from your beliefs, opinions, and needs and toward a desire to listen and learn from others. Simply put, instead of being a know-it-all leader, try the humble and vulnerable approach. Remember, every single person in your organization or team is just as important as every other. I see leaders and fellow employees look down on other team members based on job functions or titles far too often. Hierarchies like this cannot exist when you lead and encourage acting with an open mind and heart.

Psychologists have found that women are generally better than men at operating with open hearts and minds because of their motherly instincts—but I have seen some very strong male figures act in very nurturing ways, and I can assure you that it took far more courage and strength for them to act compassionately than it did for them to act dictatorial and closed off. Furthermore, the reward those men received for stepping outside their comfort zones were teams that felt motivated and excited to take on any challenges that were put in front of them. These compassionate leaders fostered a culture in which every employee in the organization was willing to work hard and long to implement and achieve very aggressive goals and actions.

As you become comfortable and confident in your own abilities to lead with an open heart and mind, your teams will remain engaged and will produce consistently effective results. Personally, I've found that those times when I've exhibited bossy, judgmental, and "always right" behaviors at work and at home have been times when I was feeling less confident in myself. I've also noticed that during these insecure times, I tend to overcompensate for my insecurity by being unwilling to listen to or appreciate others' ideas, thoughts, and feelings. It was only after going through the painful experience of feeling disconnected, lonely, and frustrated in my life that I searched out ways to improve my circumstances—and I discovered, after trying various suggested techniques, that the most effective way to create richer, more meaningful relationships is to embrace and practice being more open to others' ideas and feelings.

As you open up yourself to what others have to offer, you will become more approachable, friendly, and trustworthy. When I learned to live in the "it's not all about me, it's about them" space, my team's productivity, and my own, soared.

Interact with everyone.
Every individual in any organization adds value to the company, regardless of his or her job position, title, or salary level. There is no one person in any company who is more important than another, because the role that each person plays is an important ingredient in the recipe for solid performing results. As a people leader, it is critical that you interact with everyone on

your team for several reasons. First, this interaction demonstrates to your team members that you are approachable and accessible, and it creates a culture of trust and respect. Second, there is no better way to find out how your operation is succeeding than to see it for yourself. Third, you may find some hidden gems and leaders in areas of your organization where you least expect it.

I love the CBS show *Undercover Boss* because it demonstrates what happens when a CEO of a company works in various parts of his or her operations—undetected, in this case. It is so fun to watch how these executives interact with their teams and what they learn about the importance of all of their people. The CEOs almost always learn the power of interacting with their people by the end of the show—usually because they've gotten a new money-making or money-saving idea from a member of their organization, someone in a place they least expected it to come from. It's a great show; if you're going to explore the power of being accessible and interacting with everyone in your organization, however, I recommend doing it openly, not secretly.

Interacting in this way is often referred to as "management by walking around," and it is the only reliable way to find out how you organization is operating. I can say with 99.9 percent certainty that if you are leading from your ivory tower and expecting all the information you need to reach you through your executive team, you're fooling yourself. The information you will receive will be filtered, which means you will rarely hear the real facts or see the real results that your team is producing. Remember, people want to please their leaders, which most often means you only hear what they believe is the good news.

The best way to get the real scoop is to be with the people actually doing the work. This means you must get out of your office. Take a stroll to different departments. Talk to all levels of your organization, not just management. If you have remote organizations, take the time to pick up the phone and call them to get their views on what is going on in their world. You will be amazed at the input you get from the worker bees—and beyond that, interacting with your entire team shows them that you care about them and recognize their importance to your organization.

Being accessible to your organization lets them know you care about them. The more your team feels they matter, the more effective results they will deliver.

Being Accessible in Action

Arnold was an up-and-coming leader in Nortel. As such, he was promoted to general manager of a new products division, which was developing, manufacturing, and selling telecommunication systems to small businesses. In this role, Arnold was responsible for growing the business from zero customers and zero revenue to over twenty major customers and over $100 million in revenue over a two- to three-year period. The goals assigned to him were very aggressive, and part of this new responsibility was to create a team to help him meet these targets.

Arnold was experienced enough to know that if he was going to build this division from scratch to success quickly, he needed a team of people that would share his vision, passion, and dedication to hard work, so he carefully selected the leaders for his major departments. It took several months to get organized, but at the initial meeting with his team, Arnold made it clear to everyone that each person had a very important role in the project. He presented each goal and objective in depth, and he encouraged every team member to use his or her best talents and skills to make their division the best in the company. He also invited everyone on the team to stop by his office and share any thoughts, concerns, and ideas they had. His team left that initial meeting energized, excited, and ready for the challenge ahead of them.

Because it was a new division and they didn't have a lot of resources, most team members found themselves working ten- to twelve-hour days. Arnold was working hard himself, establishing and maintaining relationships not only with his internal team and the executive team but also with external customers and suppliers. Needless to say, he did not have a lot of free time on his hands—but Arnold recognized that in order to grow this division, it was going to take every person's talent and skills, not just his and his leadership team's. So, every day, you would find Arnold walking to each department and asking how things were going. And his employees loved it when he came around, because he was like a cheerleader. He would approach everyone with a smile and a sincere appreciation for their hard work. He would often take a moment to ask individuals how they thought things might be improved, and he was always open to hearing their new ideas. He was even known to go out into the lobby and speak with the receptionists to see how they were doing with taking calls from customers.

As customer orders started coming in, Arnold purchased a cowbell for the customer service team. He asked them to ring the bell every time a new customer order over ten thousand dollars came in. When the customer service team rang that bell, Arnold would come running from his office to high-five the customer service person who had received the order. It became a fun ritual and celebration with the team.

Arnold also stayed true to his commitment to have an open-door policy. His team was always amazed to find that when they approached him, Arnold would quickly set aside his work and invite them to come speak to him. And when they shared their thoughts, concerns, and ideas, Arnold always made them feel important. He was extremely open to listening to comments and reminding his team that in his opinion there was no such thing as a stupid idea. Arnold made every person that came to his office feel important and appreciated.

At the end of the division's first full year, all targets for customers and revenue had been exceeded. Arnold threw a party for the entire team to celebrate. During this celebration, he expressed his appreciation and gratitude to every person on his team by making an effort to personally shake hands and thank each of them face-to-face. He made a celebratory speech to the entire team, thanking them profusely for their hard work and efforts over the past year. The people on the team, meanwhile, were vocal about the fact that it was Arnold's leadership that played a big part in their desire to achieve. Arnold's commitment to being approachable, caring, and accessible to his entire team made the people who worked for him want to do their best work—not just for themselves but for him as well.

People Leadership Action Steps to Being Accessible

1. Reflect upon how accessible you currently are with your team.

2. Come up with some steps you can take to become more accessible.

3. Think of a leader you would consider accessible. What actions made him or her seem that way?

"Accessibility means leading with an open door, open heart, and open mind."

—Gina Folk

25

Value-check Policies and Processes

Doesn't it get under your skin when as a customer you hear statements from company employees like "I know that is what you want, but we don't do things like that around here" or "The reason you are not happy with our product or service is because you are not following our process" or—my all-time favorite—"It's not our policy to . . ." followed by a long list of company rules that are keeping the individual from granting your request.

When a service representative starts a conversation with me using any of these types of phrases, I want to get in his or her face and say, "Do you know who is paying your paycheck? It is me: the customer." And yet, in most of these types of situations, it is not the employee's fault that he or she cannot meet my needs. It's actually some company process or policy that prevents the individual from providing value to me; it comes from higher up.

In late 2013, I had a frustrating experience with a flight attendant on the sister airline of a company that is known for its customer service. I was heading out for vacation with my cousin, and because she was picking me up at the airport for us to drive somewhere else, I decided to carry on my bags, which consisted of a roller bag suitcase, a briefcase, and a 4 x 6–inch purse. I knew the FAA rules about carrying only *two* bags—one that would fit in the overhead bin and one that would fit below the seat—but let's be real, does a purse that practically fits in your pocket count as a bag? I didn't think so, and at least three other airport employees and authorities didn't seem to either, because I smoothly sailed through two security checks and the gate check agent with no issue.

As I merrily walked onto the plane and greeted the flight attendant nearest me with a smile, however, she authoritatively stopped me and said, "Ma'am, you are only allowed two bags. You need to consolidate your bags."

"Thanks, I know," I said nicely. "I fly your sister airline all the time, and no one has ever had an issue." I kept moving toward my seat.

"Ma'am," the flight attendant said in a tone of voice that made me think she was going to call airport security. I stopped, and she began her lecture, informing me that they were *not* their sister airline, they strictly enforced *all* rules and policies, and I needed to consolidate my bags *immediately.* This flight attendant was so bent on making me follow the rules that I held up twenty other passengers trying to board the plane as I "consolidated my bags." I was fuming and my heart was racing when I finally reached my seat. I called the customer service line of the parent company, but it was a Saturday, and they were closed. Probably a good thing.

A few days into my vacation, when I had reached a calm, relaxed, and rational state, I realized the incident was not all the flight attendant's fault. Part of the blame was mine: as the customer, I knew the rules, and I had consciously decided to break them. Part of the fault did lie with the flight attendant: she was unnecessarily rude in her enforcement of the airline's policies. She was, however, trying to do her job, which she believed required her to firmly enforce the baggage policy.

I would venture a guess that you have experienced nightmare customer service encounters like mine at some point in time—maybe even with a flight attendant. I would also bet that the majority of these bad experiences were fueled by the company's policies and processes more than they were by the individual employee. I've found that most policies and processes are created with one purpose and are never reviewed again—that is, these processes and policies are very rarely "value-checked," which means examining them to make sure there is purpose behind and benefit to them.

The reason value-checking is so important is that, under most circumstances, people are only as good as their policies and processes allow them to be. In other words, if a complicated and ineffective work method exists in your company, then no matter how talented and strong your people are, their results will not be as good as they could otherwise be.

Value-checking policies and processes to maximize workflow requires:
- Creating clear and user-friendly documentation.
- Confirming purpose and value.
- Implementing value-adding adjustments.

Create clear documentation.

The first step in performing a value check is to create clear documentation of the current state of policies and processes. In most companies, these detailed rules and procedures are stored in individual staff members' heads and do not exist in any physical form for the rest of the group to view or understand. And on the rare occasion a company does have documentation, the information is usually stored in binders with pages of detailed policies and procedures that are rarely if ever referenced or utilized by anyone.

Policies and processes can only be value-checked if they exist in a clear, easy-to-understand, and easy-to-access format. Many leaders in companies complain about how their team is not performing consistently or effectively, and yet they feel that documenting their operational guidelines and procedures is a waste of time, resources, and money. Ensuring business practices are clearly documented actually provides several benefits, however. First, it captures what really happens in your day-to-day operations, which is always an eye-opening experience. There is something about putting details in written form that immediately brings flaws, redundancies, or inadequacies in the actual policies and processes that are being carried out by your team to light. Second, clear documentation can serve as the foundation for training and communication about your day-to-day operations for current employees as well as new hires. Having this kind of uniformity in policies and processes allows each individual in your team to master his or her role more quickly and effectively, using business-wide standards instead of coworkers' versions of the workflow for reference.

Using clear documentation as your basis of operations prevents unnecessary quality issues, duplication of work efforts, and uncertainty around the proper methods in which to perform a function. And there are various ways to capture your current state. Some businesses prefer flow charts to explain their processes. Others prefer step-by-step work instructions. I have also seen a combination of flow charts and work instructions with pictorials of different aspects of a job or process. Most policies, meanwhile, are communicated in a written format. Ultimately, though, the type of documentation you create is not as critical as ensuring that your team has something to reference that empowers them to do their job in an effective manner.

You will know when your documentation is doing what it is designed to do when you find your team accessing the information on a frequent basis. If the policies and processes are created and never referred to by any team member, in contrast, then there is a problem. Most likely this lack of use would signal that the information is inaccurate, confusing, cumbersome, or out of date. Keeping documentation current is an absolute must, or there is little value in producing it the first time. If yours needs updating, assign key individuals in your team to create documentation of your current policies and process details. Encourage them to create a system that is easy for your team to access, use, and maintain; let your documented policies and processes serve as a "living representation" of the way things are currently operating. In doing so, you will set the stage for continuously value-checking your day-to-day operations.

Confirm purpose and value.

With clear and user-friendly operational documentation, you and your team can now perform a value check. The best way to confirm the value and purpose of your policies and processes is to *question everything*. Encourage your team to put every task, policy, and procedure through a thorough and detailed interrogation. Teach them to ask questions like "What is the purpose of this policy?" "What value does this process provide to the company and to our customers?" "Does the policy hinder or enhance the customer experience?" "When and from where did the process originate?" "How much cost and time does it take to enforce the policy?" "How many handoffs are there in the process?" "Is there any rework required?" "Is the process causing anyone else more work?"

While this list of questions is not exhaustive, it represents the basic premise of the Six Sigma process and quality improvement methodology that became popular in the early 2000s. The Six Sigma methodology actually teaches a practice of asking "Why?" five times in order to uncover the root cause behind any issue or concern. In my experience with interviewing process owners and employees, however, I discovered that asking "Why?" tended to put people on the defensive and very often resulted in them shutting down and preventing me from getting access to valuable information they possessed about a given situation. As I learned to be better about asking questions, I found that the information floodgates opened up, and people became more willing to share their thoughts on the processes and policies I was reviewing.

Most of my interrogations into organizations' current procedures and practices have resulted in the unearthing of at least one or two tasks or guidelines that had no inherent value to the customer or the company. The majority of these non-value-adding activities had existed for many years and were still being performed simply because no one had ever questioned the need for their use. Over the course of my career, I've personally uncovered more than fifty non-value-adding processes and policies that were costing organizations more than $100K per year to administer—and I've done it simply by asking the probing questions. Once the non-value-adding processes were identified, most of them were either eliminated or changed to deliver more value to the customers while saving money for the organization.

If you want your team to be their most profitable and effective, then make sure that there is a good understanding and reason behind every action they are asked to take.

Implement value-adding adjustments.

As you are performing value checks, you will find policies and processes that are not adding benefit to your business or the customer, and you must be willing to get rid of them. Ceasing the performance of useless activities can be difficult because it requires letting go of an attachment to the status quo—even if the status quo has been around for years. Performing an effective value check of your operations, however, makes it easier to implement value-adding adjustments for the good of staff and customers.

Uncovering and changing these non-value-adding "sleeper" policies and processes in any organization takes persistence and courage from the people that lead the groups. And the hardest policies to change are those that are not enforceable or frequently overruled.

Companies, especially big corporations, love policies. As someone who has reviewed hundreds of policies in numerous organizations, I've found that most rules are put in place to prevent a one-time problem from happening again. To make matters worse, these guidelines are frequently crafted by a governing body of individuals who have no working knowledge of their business's operations—and that makes them hard to administer and enforce in a consistent manner. Think back to my experience with the flight attendant and the carry-on bag policy. Regardless of its value, the policy is not consistently or easily enforced. Some employees are strict rule followers and enforce it, while others make their own judgment calls based on the type of carry-on. And this kind of inconsistency in enforcement creates negative situations for customers and employees.

I have also seen instances where upper management frequently overrides their staff's attempt to adhere to procedures. While there may be good reasons to not enforce the policies they do this with, these instances invalidate both the individual employee as well as the existing practice. As people leaders, when and if you discover this kind of waste, bureaucracy, and inefficiency in your organization, take the initiative to make a value-adding adjustment. Seek to understand the initial purpose behind the policy or process, and then create new and improved ways to accomplish the desired results for the business. As your team designs new solutions, urge them to create them with the customer in mind and to craft a solution that requires the least amount of overhead in time and resources.

Letting go of old, tired, non-value-adding policies and processes and replacing them with new, value-adding ones will pave the way for you, your team, and your company to be easy to do business with on a daily basis. Value-checking all your processes and policies sets the stage for your team to be their most productive and effective.

Value-checking Policies and Processes in Action

One of the key operational tools used at a large telecommunications company in the customer service and sales department was a Product Price Book. This document was the brainchild of Victor, Vice President of Operations of one of the product divisions, who felt it was important to provide customers with easily accessible details about the product portfolio, product pricing, and key ordering information.

Until Victor requested the creation of this document, customers had received product and pricing information directly from salespeople, which often meant that what they were getting was wrought with inaccuracies and outdated details. The internal ordering policies and processes had not been documented in a format that the customers and order managers could access, either—in fact, these ordering procedures had existed only in the minds of the order managers on Victor's staff.

Victor believed that having a document that would provide product and pricing information, as well as important facts and details about the customer ordering process, would make the customers' buying experience much easier and more effective, not only for the customers but for his internal department. With this in mind, he assigned the project to Norma, one of his process team members, and over the course of six months, she produced the first Product Price Book.

Upon its creation, the Price Book quickly became an important reference for communicating the product portfolio for all internal departments, including product development and management, marketing, sales, and operations. It also became customers' "bible" for placing orders. They especially loved that they could easily access the specific ordering policies and processes in the book, because up until its publication, they had to call their order management representative to learn about and understand important ordering practices.

Since the Price Book had become the company's means of communicating new and discontinued product offerings, price changes, and new marketing programs to customers, Victor gave Norma the job of making sure that the product, pricing, and customer ordering information was reviewed for accuracy and updated as needed on a monthly basis. And Norma's work was not going unnoticed: customers frequently called Victor to tell him how much they relied on the Price Book information and how critical it was to their ease of ordering for the information to be up-to-date and accurate. So, for the first two years of the Price Book's existence, Norma ensured that the information it contained was regularly reviewed, maintained, and updated with the most current product, pricing, and process details. She also checked in periodically to make sure that the customer ordering policies were still being utilized and enforced by the order management team.

As the company's product portfolio expanded, so did the reach and importance of the Price Book. It soon became apparent that they needed to maintain and distribute the information in a more automated fashion, so over the course of the next year, the Price Book was developed into an online, electronic catalog. When this change in format and organizational responsibility was made, Norma was taken off of the project.

For about five years, it seemed that the electronic format was being well maintained: customers were receiving up-to-date pricing and product information, and the company seemed to be processing customer orders with no issues. Early into the sixth year, however, Victor began receiving complaints from the customers about the same-day ordering process. In the past, they'd been able to send their orders to the customer service representative until 4:00 PM, and the orders would be entered and shipped on the same day, they told Victor; now their customer service representatives were refusing to accept same-day orders past 2:00 PM. Needless to say, they were agitated by this change.

Victor assured the customers he would investigate their concerns, and he assigned Norma the task of uncovering what had changed in the Order Management practices. Based on her prior experience, Norma knew that the original policy and processes referenced a 12:00 PM order receipt deadline to process an order the same day, so she was surprised to discover that customers had been placing orders up until 4:00 PM for years. When she went online to reference the electronic price and product catalog, she could not locate the ordering policies and process details, so she asked the team responsible for maintaining the catalog where this information was, and she discovered that they hadn't included the ordering processes and policies in the online catalog because they didn't think they were important.

Norma knew she had uncovered the first issue in the customers' concerns: lack of accessible documentation on the current policies or practices. Knowing that order management did a great job of keeping their processes and policies up-to-date internally, she requested a current version from one of the customer service representatives. With that in hand, she reviewed the same-day order process section and found that it referenced a 4:00 PM same-day order deadline. So the most up-to-date procedure document referenced the deadline the customers were expecting, but for some reason, the order managers were following a different guideline.

Norma continued to dig into the root cause of this disconnect by talking to the warehouse leader, who told her that the 4:00 PM deadline had been changed to 2:00 PM in the last two weeks because the warehouse responsible for shipping the orders had complained to the order management leader that they were receiving too many late orders and they were having to pay out a ton of overtime in order to ship these orders the same day. Out of concern for the impact on internal resources and costs, the warehouse leader and the order management leader had agreed to change the same-day ordering deadline to 2:00 PM. They had failed, however, to notify the customers of this change.

Norma reported her findings to Victor, who worked with his team to create a plan that would meet both the customers' and the company's needs moving forward. The result was threefold: First, the same-day ordering guideline was changed to 3:00 PM, a compromise that would meet both the customers' needs and the warehouse's needs. Second, Victor assigned Norma as the keeper of the order process guidelines posted in the Price Book. This meant that when a policy or process required change of any sort, the group requesting the change had to present the need to Norma, who in turn would ensure that the new process or policy would benefit both the company and the customers. Victor also requested that Norma value-check every existing procedure in the Price Book and that she consistently update and change non-value-adding or outdated policies. Third, the updated ordering policies and processes were added to the online catalog in a format that was easy for the customers and the order managers to access. This allowed the two groups to review and use the same information and ensured that customers would be notified about new guideline changes on a timely basis.

Upon implementing these improvements, customer complaints about same-day order processing disappeared, and the ordering process became a lot smoother.

People Leadership Action Steps to Value-checking Your Policies and Processes

1. Reflect upon how your processes and policies are currently documented.

2. When was the last time you value-checked your current practices? Come up with some steps you can take to perform a value check.

3. Review your processes and policies. Are there any in place that are non-value-adding?

4. Think about a time when you successfully eliminated a non-value-adding process or policy. How did that change benefit your company?

"There is nothing quite so useless as doing with great efficiency something that should not be done at all."

—Peter F. Drucker

26

Be the "Reinforcer"

To enforce or reinforce, that is the question. There are so many theories about the best way to lead individuals and teams to consistent and even superior performance. Some authorities on getting results from people believe the heavy-hand, iron-fist enforcement approach is the way to get things done, while other performance experts tout positive recognition and reinforcement methods. As a people leader, varying opinions like these can leave you in the lurch, confused about what the best practice to use with your team members really is.

When I find myself befuddled by the varying opinions I'm hearing, I sometimes look to the meaning of the key word or philosophy that is being proselytized. In the case of enforce versus reinforce, the dictionary describes the first word as *controlling*, while it describes the latter as *strengthening*. *To enforce* means "to put or keep in force, to obtain by force, to impose a course of action upon a person, or to impress or urge forcibly," while *reinforce* means "to strengthen, to make greater, to help, to support, to be responsible for, to protect, to amplify, or to encourage."

Both of these words denote getting results from an individual or team; however, the manner in which these results are achieved is very different. So think about it: Which method would personally move you to consistent and outstanding performance? Would you rather be forced to act, or do you prefer being supported and guided to greater results? I have always been fascinated by the subject of what makes humans act the way we do, and through observation, I've learned that moving people to action through reinforcement delivers longer-lasting results than does the forcing and enforcing method. People leaders who are domineering and controlling tend to get instant results from their employees—but those results are almost always "just enough" to get the leader off the employees' backs. Being an "enforcer" rarely, if ever, provides long-term and long-lasting positive results with an individual or team.

Effective people leadership is not about forcing, controlling, and intimidating people to action. Effective people leadership is about setting expectations for performance and disclosing consequences for non-performance. Being the "reinforcer" for your team members is not always just about positive reinforcement, of course; there will be times when you must follow through on stated consequences. In order to be effective, however, people leaders must understand when and how to reinforce their team members in a dynamic fashion.

As a people leader, you become the "reinforcer" by:

- Setting and resetting expectations about outcomes.
- Expecting great things from team members.
- Choosing the reinforcement method that fits the circumstances.

Set and reset expectations.

Being an effective "reinforcer" requires setting and resetting expectations. Whether an employee is new to a role or the company or has been in the role a long time, setting and resetting your expectations is a critical first step in working with him or her. Establishing expectations positively or negatively sets the future course of your team member's performance.

Setting expectations is not just about establishing rules. Although helping your employees understand your company's guidelines, policies, and rules is important to their overall performance, expectations are about achieving outcomes and the manner in which you want your team to act and behave while performing their daily activities or interacting with customers and coworkers.

Expectations may include behavior-oriented values such as honesty, integrity, presence, positive attitude, striving for personal bests, and cooperation with others. Other expectations may include what you want your team members to do when they are performing a certain task or working toward a certain goal. And a significant piece of creating expectations lies in setting out specific consequences, if there are any, if your employees' performance falls short of your expectations.

When you are setting and resetting expectations, make sure that you communicate in detail. Unfortunately, most leadership expectations are the proverbial "unwritten" type—you know, where the leader wants a team member to function in a certain manner but never actually communicates this desire out loud to that individual. I see these unexpressed expectations all the time in employee-manager relationships: the manager thinks the employee should know what he or she needs to do to perform, but the employee isn't a mind reader, so he or she doesn't understand what he or she is supposed to do. When expectations are not clearly spelled out in advance, both employees and leaders will always be disappointed with the final result. Everyone benefits when expectations are established at the very beginning of a work relationship.

Expectation-setting is not a onetime event; it must be done with every new task, project, or goal. Setting expectations must be fluid and dynamic with the changes that occur in the business or organization. In some cases, it may be appropriate to clarify expected results on a daily basis, while in others, objectives may only need to be established at the beginning of an activity, goal, or project. Whatever the situation, people can and will only perform to the level expected of them. From a performance perspective, failing to set expectations for your employees is like rolling the dice to see what results that person will deliver.

Expect great things.

One of the aspects of the "reinforcer" role is to amplify and strengthen individuals, and your effectiveness in doing so is influenced by your personal expectations of and beliefs about each individual. As a people leader, you will get what you expect from your team members—so your expectations must be solid and in alignment with one another.

Time and time again, I have seen supervisors and managers outline their expectations and *desires* for superstar performances from each of their team members in public, while what they say about the ability of these same individuals in private is in direct opposition to their stated desires. "I expect great things from every person in my organization," they tell me, "but I don't trust that Bob or Sally is capable of meeting my standards." Can you hear the absurdity in that statement? These divergent expectations mean that Bob and Sally are set up to fail before they ever begin the project at hand.

Any time I've worked with departments or organizations where the manager's desired expectations stand in polar opposition to their beliefs in their people, there has been only one outcome: subpar results. Yet the managers who have these opposing expectations of their employees are truly stumped as to why they are not performing. The bottom line is, a negative thought and a positive desire brings zero results. To get that great performance you desire from your team members, you must expect great things and believe the team can deliver outstanding results—not in theory but in *reality*. The greater your expectations of your team, the greater their potential for success.

Choose the most effective reinforcement for the situation.

Leading people is not much different than disciplining children: there is no one perfect way to do it. However, I want to make a pitch for B.F. Skinner's operant conditioning, also known as the Reinforcement Theory. This principle is defined as "an item of behavior that is initially spontaneous, rather than a response to a prior stimulus, but whose consequences may reinforce or inhibit recurrence of that behavior." Skinner found through his testing of rats that behavior could be modified based on the environment of the rats and the consequences that were applied—and he found that both positive reinforcement (giving a pleasurable response after the desired behavior is exhibited) and negative reinforcement (removing or avoiding a negative consequence when the desired behavior is exhibited) strengthened behaviors.

As a people leader, you must use your best judgment to decide when and how to apply positive versus negative reinforcement in order to shape and strengthen your team's behavior—and in order to choose the method most suitable for the situation, you must first understand the individuals with whom you are working. Self-motivated and driven employees may perform extremely well with infrequent positive reinforcement, while those team members that are unsure of themselves may require on-the-spot and frequent positive support.

In addition to understanding your team members, it is critical to understand the outcome you are trying to achieve through reinforcement. If you are trying to support a team member's achievement of a new objective, frequent positive reinforcement will be the best solution for the situation. However, if you are tackling unwanted behavioral issues or low performance, then negative reinforcement will be more effective.

When I mentor leaders, I recommend strengthening their team's performance by starting with positive reinforcement, even when they are dealing with perceived issues in performance or behavior. Nine times out of ten, positive reinforcement (over disciplinary actions) produces the longest-lasting and most outstanding results, and it's a much more rewarding experience for all parties involved.

Positive reinforcement begins with establishing your expectations for an individual's performance and then consistently rewarding his or her forward progress. This reward can be something as simple as recognition for a job well done. For instance, if your team member is expected to complete ten sales calls by eleven in the morning, then do a quick check-in at nine o'clock and congratulate him or her for making the five calls he or she has completed. Most people want to please other people and do a fantastic job, and all they need as motivation is for someone to recognize their efforts.

Positive reinforcement works most effectively when it's done with some level of frequency. When getting someone to adopt a new behavior, especially one that may be particularly challenging for him or her, recognizing progress almost every step of the way may be necessary. More self-driven or experienced individuals, meanwhile, may be comfortable with less frequent positive support.

While I would love to say that positive reinforcement works every time with great success, there will be occasions when the positive route will not take effect or deliver the results you need. In these cases, you may need to turn to the arena of negative reinforcement. You will find in business that employees, just like children, can and will take the liberty of testing boundaries and rules to see what they can get away with. I call these individuals boundary pushers; they will break a stated guideline or underperform to establish a lower expectation, and unless they experience repercussions for their actions, they will continue the undesired behavior.

Situations like these call for following through on stated consequences. Negative consequences can include eliminating bonus plans or pay raises, or even firing the employee. Whatever the consequences, negative reinforcement must be coupled with doing what you say you will do. For instance, if an individual has a history of failing to meet deadlines and has been told there will be a repercussion for continuing to perform in this manner, you must deliver on that statement. Threatening punishment and failing to follow through will only signal to your team member that you are not serious, and his or her behavior will continue. Effective people leaders tune in to their people and situations to decide which type of reinforcement will be most beneficial to the organization.

Being the "Reinforcer" in Action

As Murdoch and his leadership team were reviewing their biggest challenges for the upcoming year, one of his shift supervisors, Darin, shared his concern about absenteeism in their first-shift team. Darin shared that in the past two months, about one third of his staff had habitually called in sick on Fridays or Mondays. This attendance problem was beginning to have an impact on the team's ability to deliver and ship customer orders, so Darin asked Murdoch for his guidance on how to fix the issue.

Murdoch asked Darin to describe the steps he had taken with his team up until that point to improve their attendance at work. Darin said he had reported the offending employees to their on-site human resources representative and that their attendance was being documented—but he admitted that no real action had been taken with each person. Murdoch reminded him that as shift supervisor, it was his responsibility to change his team's performance and behavior, not human resources'. Darin said he was uncertain about how to move forward, so Murdoch agreed to help him craft an improvement plan.

The next day, Darin and Murdoch met to discuss solutions. Murdoch asked Darin to articulate his attendance expectations for his team, and as Darin stammered and stuttered his way through his explanation, Murdoch saw the first challenge: Darin could not even articulate his expectations for his team's being on time and present for work. He was not certain how many days a person could miss or be late to work in a specific time period without consequences, and he was even less sure of what the actual negative impact of his employees' failure to meet expectations was. Darin explained that absenteeism had never been a problem before, so he was not well versed in what he expected.

As a first step, Murdoch asked Darin to set his expectations for his team's being on time and present at work. And in creating these expectations,

Murdoch suggested that Darin become very clear on the consequences for not adhering to the guidelines he created. Darin did as Murdoch suggested, and within a week of their initial meeting, he had established clear expectations and associated consequences for non-performance that had been blessed by the human resources team. Murdoch suggested that Darin communicate these expectations with his team and then give them some time to see if their attendance improved.

After about three weeks, Darin noticed that the attendance problem was actually getting worse. He approached Murdoch once again and shared that while he wanted his team to be on time and show up for work, he really doubted whether this group of employees he had could ever live up to his expectations. Many of them were young, and he had heard through the grapevine that many of them were telling friends and coworkers that they were missing so much work because they were partying on their free time.

After listening to Darin, Murdoch pointed out the existence of his personal misalignment of expectations and asked him if he thought he could change his perspective. Darin said he would try. Murdoch also recommended that Darin stop focusing on the behavior that was upsetting to him and start focusing on the positive behaviors of his top offenders. He suggested that Darin go out of his way to profusely thank the offending employees when they did show up on Fridays and Mondays as soon as they walked through the door and to tell them how glad he was to see them at work and how grateful he was that they were there to help the team achieve their goals. He reminded Darin to also reinforce positive attendance in other team members in front of the offenders so everyone on his shift could see positive recognition being consistently applied. Darin agreed to implement both of Murdoch's solutions with his team right away.

Much to his surprise, Darin's actions worked: in less than a month, just by changing his expectations and offering positive recognition for his team for their presence at work, Darin saw a drastic improvement in his employees' attendance.

People Leadership Action Steps to Being the "Reinforcer"

1. Think about how your team would describe you. Would they call you an enforcer or "reinforcer"?

2. List some things that you do to support and strengthen your team today.

3. Come up with some steps you can take to provide more reinforcement for your group.

4. Describe the traits and actions of a "reinforcer" you admire.

"Without a doubt, providing recognition is one of the best ways (if not the best way) to build and maintain superior performance. The reason for that is quite simple: reinforced behavior gets repeated."

—Eric Harvey

27

Master Your Mindset

An individual's mindset has to do with how fixated a person is on a certain attitude or thought. I am a firm believer in the concept that one's mind dictates one's actions and results in one's personal and professional life. There is a story about two salesmen who were sent to a developing country by their company, a shoe manufacturer, to investigate the market potential for selling shoes there. Each of them spent time observing and engaging with the local citizens to determine what kind of shoe needs the people there might have, and upon returning from their trip, each salesman reported his findings back to their manager. One of the salesmen lamented to his boss that the people in that country did not wear shoes, and as a result, there was little hope for growth there. The other salesman, in contrast, was overflowing with excitement about the possibilities in this country; he said that based on his conversations and findings, the people there had never had the opportunity to communicate their needs and desires for shoes, and there was *massive* potential there for a shoe company willing to listen.

This story of two very different perspectives is a perfect example of how mindset influences outcomes in life. The potential for selling shoes varied dramatically here—from zero to massive—with just a slight shift in mindset.

Mindset demonstrates how you see and operate in the world. The good news is that it's a choice: you get to decide whether to view a situation, decision, or relationship in a positive or negative light. As a people leader, your mindset has a strong influence on your team and their performance, so it's important to learn how to master it. Mindset is not something we are born with—it's a skill that must be learned. To master it is a process that requires effort and practice.

Mastering your mindset as a people leader requires:

- Being aware of how others perceive your mindset.
- Responding versus reacting.
- Striving for optimism.

Be aware of how others perceive your mindset.

As a people leader, your team measures your effectiveness with every conversation you have and every decision you make. After all, you are in charge, and that means your people rely on your vibe, view, and reactions to the current state of the organization as a guide to how they should think and react. Understanding your team's perceptions of how you come across in your conversations and actions is critical for mastering your mindset.

I learned about the importance of perceptions the hard way several times over the course of my leadership career. I tend to think of myself as a positive, confident, and optimistic individual. I see the good in most situations and outcomes that I encounter, even when they appear negative. I expect greatness from myself and every person I meet, and I truly believe that people can accomplish things far greater than they think they can. I view myself as having an empowering and positive mindset and nature. However, there have been times during my career when I've been informed that people have felt intimidated by me. The first time I heard this, I was flabbergasted. I could not imagine why or how anyone could be intimidated by me. And yet, as I dug deeper into the perception, I discovered that I scared some of my team members because of my positive outlook and expectations. Many of these individuals had never encountered a leader like me before. They were used to "realists" or dictators, and my "we can do anything" mindset and energy unnerved them.

Your team's perception of your mindset is their reality, and knowing what that perception is can give you clues about how and where you may need to make some personal adjustments. In my case, I learned that while I was not going to shift away from my positive and optimistic mindset, it might help if I toned down my approach ever so slightly. I've seen other cases where managers who claim to be optimistic and upbeat often talk to their staff about how concerned they are about the current and future state of the organization or company. Leaders like this might benefit from tempering any concerns they might want to share with some degree of positivity. Seeing how others perceive your mindset is a critical starting point for mastering your mindset.

Respond; don't react.

Mastering your mindset is about intentionally choosing how and what to think. That means you must take a little time to consider the facts and weigh options before you act. Unfortunately, for those of us in leadership positions, taking time to intentionally respond sometimes feels impossible. We feel pressured to react to requests and often shoot back quick responses without taking the time to understand what is being asked of us. But reacting is almost always going to result in a negative outcome when it comes to leading people. If you are like me, you don't have enough toes and fingers to count the number of times you've wished you had taken just five minutes to respond to a request or statement instead of reacting in thirty seconds or less—because it's often resulted in me having to spend hours cleaning up my mess, re-explaining what I meant to say, repairing injured relationships, and setting up a positive "go forward" plan. All that wasted time could have been saved, and all those emotions and efforts could have been spared, if I had simply listened, processed, and chosen my response wisely instead of dashing off a quick reply.

We have been programmed by parents, teachers, bosses, and society to give quick answers, so much so that we have lost the art of mindful and intentional responses. Mastering your mindset is about mastering the art of responding conscientiously. It's not a difficult thing to do; in fact, it is quite simple. The process of intentional response begins with the simple step of taking time to pay attention to what others are saying, whether verbally or in writing. How often have you sent an e-mail or text only to receive a response that made it clear that the recipient had not taken the time to really read or understand what you had requested? Frustrating, right? Well, when you receive a verbal or written request, the first step to responding intentionally is to listen to what the individual is saying. And by listening, I mean paying attention—to the words, to the facts, and also to the tone.

If you have a tendency to skim over things, you can focus your attention by writing down, highlighting, reading, and rereading key points in the communications you receive prior to responding. Staying actively involved and focused on the request or communication enables you to refrain from quickly acting on emotions and preconceived answers and thoughts. The next step in mindfully responding is to parrot back to the individual(s) what you have heard or read to confirm that you have not added any personal perceptions or misconceptions to the information the individual was conveying. With your understanding of the issue validated, you can now choose how to respond in an educated and non-emotional manner.

Your responses will be most effective when they are in alignment with the facts presented, consider all parties involved in the situation, and enable a positive outcome for the organization. When you master the art of responding versus reacting, you will be one step closer to mastering your mindset.

Strive for optimism.

As you decide how to respond to any situation, I encourage you to strive for a positive slant. To borrow some well know clichés—see the glass as half full instead of half empty, or think of the day as mostly sunny rather than partly cloudy. This matters because presenting a situation in a positive manner is the number one thing you can do to prevent panic and anxiety in an organization.

When I recommend the "optimism" approach to managers, some of them reply that they are realists, and that it's important for their team to understand the facts—they don't want to sugarcoat things. I agree that facts are always important to share, but I would also argue that the way in which you present the meaning of those facts has a huge influence on your team. Remember, your employees are going to look to how you feel about and represent a situation to determine how they are going to act. If you choose to report facts with a blaming, accusatory, doomsday attitude, your team will feel dejected and will feel little motivation to make the situation better in the future. If you present the not-so-pleasant facts as simply those—facts—and encourage your team to come up with solutions for resolving and improving the situation, in contrast, they will feel like they're part of the solution.

When I give my teams bad news, I like to deliver it with the following message: "While the facts may seem bleak, the good news is that each and every one of us has a choice as to what to make this information mean. We can choose to see it as a sign that we are destined for failure and should just give up, *or* we can see it as a message that what we have been doing up until now has not worked and we need to either stop doing it or improve it going forward."

The only way I know to maintain forward progress is to see a situation for what it is right now and move forward with a positive attitude. When you strive for optimism rather than pessimism as a people leader, you will find that your results will be far more effective.

Mastering Your Mindset in Action

Fiona was sitting at her desk one day, fuming with frustration and anger. Her boss, Irene, had just informed her that the budget for the major system project Fiona's team was leading had been cut by over $75,000—and the project completion target date had been moved forward by six weeks. Fiona's mind was racing with concerns, fears, and questions about how she and her team were going to pull off this seemingly impossible challenge.

This was the third time management had changed their expectations about Fiona's team's critical projects in the past year, and she was over it. She could only think of the reasons why her team was going to fail under the new directive, as well as the fact that her team was already working long hours and weekends on this project and now she had to tell them that they had to work even harder, and with less.

Dreading sharing the news, but knowing she had to do it, Fiona sent her entire team a terse e-mail commanding each of them to attend a mandatory conference call. In her e-mail, she made it clear that no excuses would be accepted for missing the meeting. Her tone was less than positive, and as her team members read her message, they began panicking and calling one another to speculate about the subject of the meeting, creating their own versions of what they believed was going to take place in their session. It was clear from the tone of Fiona's e-mail that she was angry, and they couldn't figure out why that might be the case; the team's last project update with Fiona had been very positive.

By the time Fiona's team dialed into the conference call, they were all worried and perplexed about what was going on. And Fiona's tone did nothing to reassure them: she was quiet and was not responding to questions in her normal welcoming and encouraging way. Her team was used to her positive attitude and bubbly personality, so her terseness and distant energy made them even more nervous and concerned.

When the entire team was present on the call, Fiona shared the news of the $75,000 budget cut and the change in the project completion date. She also provided her own personal commentary about the situation, telling her team that she thought management was "out of their minds" to set such ridiculous objectives. She told them all that she was frustrated and did not feel motivated to meet the new standards.

The more Fiona talked, the more the task at hand seemed impossible to achieve. Her comments left her entire team feeling scared, overwhelmed, and let down. They could not believe the pressure the executives were putting on them; it felt like just another unachievable edict demanded of the team from the "powers that be." They joined Fiona's pity party, full of complaints and concerns about how the changes would negatively impact their work and personal performance—and the more they ranted and raved, the more fearful and anxious they all became.

After about forty-five minutes of discussion, Fiona decided it was time to get back to work. She closed the call by requesting her team to stay focused on the project tasks and do what they could to achieve the new goals. By that time, however, Fiona's team was convinced that they could not possibly complete the project with $75,000 and six weeks less than expected. They were all convinced that the project and their roles were doomed for utter failure.

At the end of this challenging workday, Fiona left feeling exhausted and ready to quit. She genuinely did not want to return to work the next day—or ever, for that matter. In order to unwind from the madness her workday, she followed her normal ritual of eating dinner and then relaxing with a book and a nice glass of wine. She was having a hard time focusing on reading her book, however; she was still fuming about and replaying the events of the last few days, her thoughts full of all the "he said, she said" conversations she'd had with her team members and the executives.

Frustrated and tired, Fiona went to bed—but still her mind would not stop the replay. She kept running through every scenario in her mind, trying to make management the "bad guys" for demoralizing her team. In the wee hours of the morning, however, after having gotten little to no sleep all night, Fiona heard an internal whisper that reminded her that her team had surmounted far more difficult challenges in the past.

With this thought, Fiona finally fell asleep, and when she awoke the next day, she felt embarrassed and ashamed by her behavior toward her team and the executives. She reminded herself that she was a leader and was therefore responsible for her team's behavior. And she knew that the *one* thing she could control in this situation was her attitude.

Fiona went to work that morning feeling driven to make the project a success and to improve the negative working environment her attitude had set into motion. She sent out an e-mail first thing asking her employees to join her for another conference call to discuss the project challenge—but this time, instead of being negative, her e-mail was full of possibility and encouragement and requested that her team join her to brainstorm how they could meet the challenge.

Fiona's team joined the call feeling somewhat confused by Fiona's quick change in attitude from the previous day, but ready to brainstorm. Before they began, Fiona apologized to all of them for her negative approach on the previous call. She explained that she had been taken off guard by the executives' request and that she had overreacted. She acknowledged that her attitude was less than encouraging and had caused unnecessary fear and frustration within the team, and—reminding everyone that they had achieved far greater challenges on past projects—she assured them that they could excel on this project as well. Then she asked them to join her in approaching the challenge of the budget cut and date change with a fresh mindset.

After a few rounds of positive brainstorming, Fiona's team created several ideas for how they could cut the budget and meet the new timeline. They decided that by simply eliminating and postponing a few of the "nice to have, but not required" software features they had planned to include, the project budget and timeline deliverables could be achieved with ease. Fiona and her team left the call feeling upbeat and ready to take on and achieve the new challenge.

After a few weeks of focused, hard work, Fiona's team completed their project and met the revised stretch objectives. Not only did they reduce their spending by the required $75,000, the project was also implemented within one week of the expected date. As Fiona reported her team's results back to Irene, she reflected on how her attitude had turned out to be a key driver for her team's success. Without her attitude adjustment, her team performance could have been disastrous—but instead, both she and her team had met the challenge with a positive attitude and energy, and their efforts had paid off.

People Leadership Action Steps to Mastering Your Mindset

1. Think about your mindset at work. If I asked each member of your team what your mindset is, how would they respond?

2. Come up with some steps you can take to respond versus react in your daily activities.

3. Do you consider yourself a glass-half-full or glass-half-empty person? Think about whether your team members would agree with that assessment.

4. Think about a time when you gave yourself an attitude adjustment that had a positive impact on you and your organization. What happened?

"Everything can be taken from a man or a woman but one thing: the last of human freedoms—to choose one's attitude in any given set of circumstances, to choose one's own way."

—Viktor Frankl

28
Have Fun

According to a 2009 survey done by the American Psychological Association, 69 percent of workers say that work is a significant source of their stress, and 41 percent of those individuals report feeling stressed out at work. In that same survey, 51 percent of employees said they are less productive because of stress. In 2001, P.J. Rosch from the American Institute of Stress reported that job stress is estimated to cost U.S. companies more than $300 billion a year in absenteeism, turnover, diminished productivity, and medical and other administrative costs. With numbers like these, it is no wonder that companies are looking for new and innovative ways to reduce stress.

One of the best stress reducers I've found in my years in business is to have fun. Whenever I think of fun, I am reminded of Cyndi Lauper's epic song, "Girls Just Wanna Have Fun." But really, that's true for everyone—not just girls. We *all* just wanna have fun. And since most of us work a minimum of eight hours a day and usually more like ten to twelve, why wait until after work to do it?

I've often wondered when in history it was decided that work and business had to be sooo serious. I suspect it started because some authority was certain that work could not be mixed with play; however, according to Dr. Stuart Brown, founder of the National Institute for Play, "There is good evidence that if you allow employees to engage in something they want to do, (which) is playful, there are better outcomes in terms of productivity and motivation." Brown goes on to say that "play can also lower your stress levels, boost your optimism, and increase your motivation to move up in a company and improve concentration and perseverance. There's some evidence from animal studies that engaging in play opens up new neural connections in the brain, leading to greater creativity. All sorts of creative new connections are made when you're playing that otherwise would never be made."

Some of the largest corporations are instilling fun in their culture. Google employees can play beach volleyball, go bowling, or scale a climbing wall at their headquarters in California. Southwest flight attendants and crew members are encouraged to pepper in their personal version of fun throughout their daily activities—decorating their gates for holidays, singing their way through in-flight announcements, playing roll-the-toilet-paper up and down the aisles during long flights, or making the customers laugh during safety briefing announcements. Other companies provide Ping-Pong tables or arcade games for their employees to use when they need a break from the long day.

As a people leader, there are a number of simple ways you and your team can have fun. It does not always require a huge investment of money or time—and if there is even the slightest possibility that having fun will decrease stress and increase productivity, why not try it?

You can have more fun at work by:

- Creating fun in the most mundane tasks.
- Making time to laugh.
- Holding fun activities during and after work hours.

Create fun out of the mundane.

Let's face it, making a business run smoothly is not always interesting or exciting. Sometimes work activities are tedious, boring, mundane, and repetitive, so much so that individuals can lose their zest to perform and even their desire to come to work every day. Peppering a little amusement into a routine every now and then can actually ignite your team members' participation. For one thing, fun serves as a process interrupt; people often function on autopilot and are not even aware of their efforts or the quality of their work, and creating a fun diversion in the midst of an otherwise monotonous activity can give them a fresh new perspective about the work.

The practice of adding a little lightheartedness to a task can actually inspire your employees to find new and creative ways of doing things or can serve as a catalyst to focus on providing good service. Breaking the monotony of a job by infusing a little fun in it and shaking up the routine can inspire your team members with renewed excitement and passion for their roles.

There are numerous ways to infuse fun into boring assignments. One approach is to create friendly competitions for individuals or teams. For instance, if one of your team members has to scan a bunch of documents into your online storage system, set milestones and give her silly little prizes for achieving each milestone. Maybe she can usually complete twenty scans an hour. Why not give her a gold star for processing thirty an hour? After accumulating a certain amount of stars, you could allow her to choose from an assortment of inexpensive games or toys. Have you ever watched how much money people sink into carnival games trying to win a cheap stuffed animal? Why not institute the same kind of concept at work? In my experience, the "cheesier" the game and the prize, the more fun it is for your team members because it brings out the child in them.

You can also create friendly competitions between teams, where the winning team wins the prize of their choice. If you are unsure what your team members think is fun, ask them for their own creative ideas on how to make their day-to-day activities more enjoyable.

Make time to laugh.

I once heard a stunning statistic: kids laugh 300 to 400 times a day, while adults only laugh fifteen. What a bummer. Not only has laughter been proven to be good for your physical health, it has been demonstrated that it helps individuals be more productive in the workplace. Good people leaders understand that laughter really is the best medicine when it comes to their employees' well-being.

You don't have to be a comedian to make your team members chuckle. There are several great ways to generate merriment without the use of jokes. If your team is faced with a pressing, stressful situation, for example, you can take time to make light of the issue. You might do this by creating a tall tale about the situation. In the heat of a stressful moment, take a break and begin creating the story—"Once upon a time, there was . . ."—and ask each team member to add details for the plot. As hokey as this exercise sounds,

I actually have tried it with teams, and you'd be surprised at how engaged people get and how quickly it can defuse a tense situation.

Another way to lighten things up at work is to take time out of a busy day to have a laugh break. Gather your team and ask them to just start laughing. If they are resistant, start it off yourself by laughing. Laughter is extremely contagious. I've chuckled on conference calls and waited for people to ask me, "Gina, what's so funny?"—to which I would respond, "Oh nothing, I just thought we needed a laugh." Without fail, this always made my team start laughing themselves. This also works when you've made a mistake. If, instead of getting angry and frustrated with yourself, you take just a few moments to chortle at your mistake, you will get an instant release of stress and a new and refreshed energy and attitude about the situation. Some of my best solutions have come to me after taking a "laugh out" moment.

However you do it, finding ways to create laughter with your team will increase their energy, spark creativity, and boost morale. More importantly, laughing is just fun!

Host fun activities inside and outside work.

Team fun in and outside the workplace should be encouraged and supported. Very often, I hear managers complain that taking time to have fun is an unproductive use of resources—and after they stop whining, I tell them to do it anyway. Allowing your team to participate in fun activities generates a lot of positive energy and builds loyalty and camaraderie within your team. Fun also establishes a sense of belonging and community in the work environment that motivates people to engage and perform at their best. I've encouraged every team I've worked with throughout my career to find new ways to have fun.

When I was managing one of my more creative project teams, my team suggested having a weekly fun hour. Since we were dispersed across the United States and Canada, we had to find a way to have fun together in a remote manner. We could not just go out to a movie or have a party in person, so we had to get creative. My team crafted a brilliant solution: each week, one member was assigned to lead a fun game or activity that we could do over the phone or via the Web. The creativity was incredible. We played childhood games like Hangman, Family Feud, and Name that Tune through web conferences, and we got to know each other by engaging in a

"Who Am I" game where we shared personal facts and pictures of ourselves. The team looked forward to this excitement each week, and they told me that hour was the motivation they needed to get them through their stressful deliverables each day.

For those teams who are all together onsite, you might try creating fun committees—employee teams whose sole purpose is to find out what their team members want to do for fun during and after work. We had costume parties, collected and delivered food at Thanksgiving to families in need, and held a carnival with a dunking booth in which all the managers were the "dunkees." Over the years, I came to realize that it didn't really matter what the activity was—it was the infusion of fun into the work environment, whatever its form, that boosted employee happiness, creativity, and productivity.

Bring more fun to your workplace, and have fun watching your results!

Having Fun in Action

One team I was responsible for during my time at Nortel was a group in charge of implementing a new supply chain system that integrated the order management, inventory, purchasing, and warehouse and distribution functions and processes into one platform. One year we had an assignment so significant that it was one of the key deliverables on the general manager's objectives for the year. Because of the visibility and importance of the project, the expectations and pressure to perform were extremely high.

We selected a team of six dedicated, top-performing project managers—a fairly small group for a project of this magnitude and scope—to tackle the task. The team knew in advance that they were going to have to work a minimum of sixty hours a week, including frequent weekend work, for eight months in order to meet their deadlines. They were ready for the task at hand, but I knew it was going to be a long, tough road—and I also recognized that it was my responsibility to come up with creative ways to keep their energy and creativity high and their stress as low as possible throughout the project so we could meet our project milestones.

The first thing we did was take an old conference room and turn it into our own project room. This was a place where all of us gathered to work side by side, testing system features, writing process documentation, or brainstorming about how to best implement process changes throughout the various teams to support the system transition. I encouraged the team to make this room their own since they were going to be spending an enormous amount of time there over the next eight months. I was surprised at how much fun the team had adding their personal touches to the room; in no time, it had been transformed from a sterile conference room to a place that exuded creativity and comfort.

One of the first additions to the room was an endless supply of energy, fun, and *candy!!!* One of our team members committed to bringing in some new treat for us each week. It was hysterical to watch seven adults, including me, anxiously await the new supply of candy every Monday. I felt like a kid at Halloween, buzzing with excitement about the different candy offered at each house.

Another team member took it upon herself to post weekly and sometimes daily positive quotes and motivational pictures. Some days the quotes would be just what we needed to get us through one more day of the pressure-cooker demands of the project. On other days, the comic strips or funny pictures of strangers doing stupid things she posted gave us all a much-needed laugh.

I encouraged the team to take breaks when they felt their energy was waning or their creativity was stalled, and we soon instituted a process where, if the team mood got too intense or the energy seemed too low, someone would say, "Time for a break! Let's go outside for a walk!" or maybe "Does anyone have any funny stories? I need a laugh." The team recognized the importance of clearing their heads, and they made it a priority to catch a few moments of amusement to separate from the stress of the day on a regular basis. They rarely paused their work for more than fifteen minutes, and they got some of their best work done shortly after their return from these power fun breaks.

Because I was the project leader, I frequently had to travel to various locations to provide progress reports on the system project to other operations leaders whose teams were going to be impacted by the change. This meant that at least once a month I was traveling to other company locations across the United States and Canada. When I traveled, I always made a point to call my team at the project room to make sure they were progressing and to find out if they needed my support for anything. Most of the time when I called, the team was feeling energetic and motivated; however, one week, I could tell they were feeling down, discouraged, and burned out.

If I were there, I could do something fun and goofy with them that would make them laugh—but I knew I could not have the same effect over the phone, so I needed to come up with a different tactic.

I decided to call my mom and ask her to help me out. She was also working at Nortel at the time—she was on the sales and marketing team—so she knew all of my team members and could empathize with how stressful our work challenges were these days. I told her my team needed some renewed energy and that I wanted to infuse something fun into their workday, and then I asked her to go to the Dollar Store with twenty dollars and buy bags full of fun toys for the team.

The next day, my mom went into the project room and dumped the bags of toys and games she had purchased onto the project room table. There were bubbles, coloring books and crayons, paddleballs, puzzles, a gumball machine, a kaleidoscope, game cards, toy guns, toy soldiers, and jacks, to name a few. When she called me afterward, my mom told me that my team's energy shifted immediately when they saw the toys and games—and when I returned from my trip, my team excitedly and happily relayed their version of the experience. I could tell that taking time to have a little fun had boosted their creativity and energy because since our call, they had completed a critical round of testing that had been on their plates for one week.

My team continued their efforts on the project for the next four months, and I'm proud to say that they had complete success in implementing the supply chain system per the project and budget expectations. Our general manager was extremely pleased with our work and rewarded the team with nice bonuses for their efforts!

That project and team taught me the importance of having fun in the workplace. My team continued our quest for fun with every project we were assigned going forward—and because we took time to enjoy ourselves as we were working, we made a name for ourselves as being one of the most productive project teams in the operations department.

People Leadership Action Steps to Having Fun

1. Think about what your team's day-to-day is like. What do you do to have fun at work?

2. Come up with some activities you and your team can engage in to generate a little fun for yourselves every day.

3. Think of the most fun and successful work environment you've worked in. What made it so fun?

"People rarely succeed unless they have fun in what they are doing."

—Dale Carnegie

29
Recharge Your Battery

As a leader, your days are filled with demands from pressing deadlines, hoards of people requesting your time, various meetings, customer issues, budget numbers to meet, reports, calls, and projects. You most likely have a to-do list that could keep you and your team busy for months or even years. Just thinking about what needs to get done probably makes you exhausted. Each one of these activities can suck the energy right out of you like vampires suck blood from their prey—and if you're not careful, they can leave you just as lifeless.

You may dream of being swept off your feet to a tropical island with no phones, computers, or people, but as nice as that might sound, you know you still have a job to do. The only way to press on without killing yourself is to find a way to renew your energy so you can be at your best every day. Just think about Iron Man, the Marvel superhero. He can run at full steam, accomplishing great things and ridding the world of evil—and after each one of his heroic adventures, he has to come home and recharge himself so he can continue to do great work. As a people leader, you are not that different from Iron Man. In order to sustain your performance and remain effective, you must recharge *your* battery. No matter who you are, you need energy and mental clarity to be at the top of your game.

People leaders take time to recharge their batteries by:
- Maintaining a well-rounded lifestyle.
- Igniting others.
- Disengaging and relaxing.

Maintain a well-rounded lifestyle.

Magazine and newspaper articles, blog postings, and news clips constantly remind us of the importance of living a healthy lifestyle. Not a day goes by without some new theory coming out about how eating a healthy diet, exercising, and getting seven to nine hours of sleep a day are important to sustaining energy and activity levels. And few disagree with these theories: a healthy body is extremely important and is one of our major sources of energy. But being healthy is about more than physical health.

To live a well-rounded life you must have a synergistic mix of physical health, emotional health, and spiritual health. Many of us have heard this kind of living referred to as a "well-balanced" life. I prefer the term "well-rounded" to "well-balanced," however, because the word "rounded" suggests that all parts have to be in equal proportion to make our lives whole. The wheel of a vehicle cannot function effectively when its air is not distributed evenly, and this applies to our lives as well. We need strong physical, emotional, and spiritual health in order to achieve our greatest energy and clarity.

I have learned in life that I must attend to my physical, emotional, and spiritual health in order to function at my highest potential and achieve outstanding results. With that in mind, I replenish and maintain my physical health with a diverse exercise regimen and by drinking plenty of water and eating the right foods (at least most of the time). Emotional energy is different, though. My emotional energy generates from being challenged and making a difference in my work, being of service to others, and spending a lot of fun time with friends and family. And I am at my best when I try to use both sides of my brain. I am definitely a left-brainer, driven and analytical, so every now and again I try something creative to exercise my right brain. I have been known to pull out a coloring book and just start coloring like a kid to activate my right hemisphere. When I am feeling emotionally down, meanwhile, I can snap right out of it by focusing on my favorite things and on the positive aspects of my life. No matter how bad a day I am having, thinking of just one positive thing will spark a smile in me.

Last and certainly not least in my well-rounded life is my spiritual practice. I know from personal experience that I can do far more for myself and others when I put my faith in a higher spiritual power source. For me, knowing that I am not alone and that there is a higher power with me at all times gives me a tremendous amount of energy. I engage in quiet contemplation and gratitude throughout my day. Just looking at something in nature reminds me that I am just a small piece of the larger world and that I am not alone.

For me, living a well-rounded life gives me the perfect mix of quiet and electricity that I need to be most effective in my personal and professional life. And don't forget, when you're a people leader, people not only rely on you, they *watch* you. Showcasing a well-rounded lifestyle gives others in your world silent permission to do the same for themselves. That's why effective people leaders are in tune with the fact that their true source of energy, strength, and clarity originates from a well-rounded lifestyle.

Ignite others.

Throughout the year, and especially during the holidays, we are bombarded with the age-old teaching "It is better to give than to receive." It may seem like a cliché at this point, but it's true: giving and igniting energy in others is a great way to relight your own flame. This is only true, however, when it is done out of a sense of giving and not responsibility. Many of us feel drained because our so-called "free time" feels like it is spent giving to others.

If you are a busy mom or dad, you probably rush home from work each day to take care of your kids. Or maybe you have an aging parent who requires your help, or maybe you have a pet that requires your love and care. Taking care of our loved ones is important, of course—but did you notice the word "give" is not in the phrase "taking care"? The type of giving I am referring to is that which has no strings or responsibilities attached to it. Giving can be simple, like complimenting your coworker or doing a favor for someone when he or she did not expect it. When you give lovingly and unconditionally to others, you not only provide them a source of positive energy, you also give yourself an instant boost.

One of the games I like to play is the "smile at everyone" game. No matter where I am or who I see, I simply smile and then watch what happens. Most children reciprocate with a huge toothy grin and sometimes a chuckle. Adults, on the other hand, are a mixed bag. Some return the smile while others scowl at you and make you feel like you are crazy! When I receive a positive response from adults and children, I get an instant charge of energy. And when the response is less positive, I tell myself that the person is probably having a bad day, and at least I acknowledged his or her presence, which makes me feel good.

Another "no strings attached" method of igniting others is to express your appreciation and gratitude for something they've done. You can express it in person, or in writing, or even privately, just by thinking about the person. Whatever your method, consciously feeling and expressing gratitude for someone's or something's presence in your life generates a huge amount of energy for both you and the recipient.

I encourage you to find simple ways that work for you to ignite the energy in others in your life.

Disengage and relax.

For many people leaders, disengaging and relaxing seems impossible and counterintuitive to their driven-to-achieve natures. Relaxing may sound like torture to some; for others, it may just sound like an impossible luxury because of all the demands on their time. But disengaging and relaxing is critical to avoiding physical and mental burnout.

Many of us think about vacation as our means of unwinding and letting go. With today's digital world, however, many people don't ever unplug—not even on vacation. The kind of disengaging and relaxing I'm talking about is taking a real time-out and stepping off the proverbial gerbil wheel of our busy lives, even if it is just for a brief moment or two. Simple activities like taking five to ten minutes out of a busy, stressful day to just close your eyes and focus on breathing can rejuvenate your mind and body. In many Latin cultures, businesses close for an hour or two around lunchtime, allowing their employees to take a siesta in order to regain their energy for the rest of the day. Fifteen- to twenty-minute power naps have been scientifically proven to be a great way to restore clarity and focus. Many companies have recognized the importance of taking breaks and have peppered meditation or yoga times throughout the day for their team members. Other businesses have added nap rooms for workers who feel like they need to get a little mental refresher.

What's important to note here is that more and more organizations are recognizing the importance of allowing employees to take quick time-outs throughout a workday to disengage, clear the mind, and relax. As a people leader, it's your job to serve as the example and then empower your team to follow suit. Pick the method that works best for you and your team culture, and then make time to relax and disengage consistently throughout the workday.

Another thing you can do to help yourself relax is to leave work when you leave work. This means doing your best not to take work home with you, physically or mentally. Being a workaholic is just as serious an addiction as any other substance abuse; it may be more expected or accepted in today's day and age, but work will eventually destroy you and those around you if you are not able to disengage from it. When you leave work, take time to enjoy your personal life. Spend quality time with your family, pets, and friends doing what you love to do. Plug into other sources of energy besides work that are fun to you. People leaders who take time to disengage and relax will marvel at the amount of energy and sharpness doing so brings to themselves and others in their world.

People leadership requires a lot of energy. It is critical to do what you need to do in order to recharge every day. Encourage your team members to do the same for themselves. Share your energy-generating practices with your team, and inspire them to make their own personal time to reenergize. Everyone functions more effectively and efficiently when they are refueled and recharged!

Recharging Your Battery in Action

When I began my career, I was fresh out of college. I entered the workforce ready to take on any opportunity or challenge that came my way. My parents had taught me that hard work and dedication were the way to achieve success in my life; for me, this meant that I gave 110 percent and stayed late at work until the job at hand was done. In the first ten years of my career, I spent most of my waking hours at work. Most weekdays, I was the first person to arrive and one of the last people to leave the office. My work was challenging and fun, and I loved it; I was very much energized by my accomplishments on the job.

On some occasions, my coworkers and I would go out after our long day to relax and have a little fun. However, even when we vowed not to talk about it, most of our conversations crept back to work; that's what we had in common, after all. As for vacations, forget it—there was no time. I actually bragged that I had not had a vacation in years and wore that fact like some sort of merit badge. When my body tried to tell me to slow down by getting sick, I just kept pressing on and worked through and around whatever ailed me. My brain never slowed down. I was eating, drinking, and sleeping my job, twenty-four hours a day.

The hard work and focus paid off, just like my parents told me it would. Promotion after promotion came my way. I got frequent salary boosts and stock option grants. Things were looking pretty awesome, from my point of view. My multitasking skills were so strong that I ended a ten-year romantic relationship, got an MBA, found a new man, and got married during this five-year period of my life. I was busy, busy, busy, and I truly felt like I was on fire, soaring to new heights. I was certain that work was my source of power and energy.

Unbeknownst to me, other parts of my life were silently and gradually falling apart. Mental and physical exhaustion were catching up with me. My patience with people was dwindling, and I've been told that I was a nightmare to be around, although I had no idea that was how I was showing up around people at the time. My employees, peers, family, and friends walked around on eggshells wondering if they were going to be the next victim of my frustration and aggravation. My physical health suffered too: I had little to no time to exercise or eat healthfully, and I was twenty-five pounds overweight. My spiritual practice, meanwhile, was nonexistent. My Sundays were reserved for the "Church of St. Mattress" because I was too tired and disinterested in going anywhere.

The more personally dissatisfied and unhappy I felt, of course, the more I poured myself into work. I still thought my energy came from working, and if I just worked more, things would improve. My wakeup call didn't come until I was faced with a failed marriage and a stalled career. I had hit rock bottom. I remember one weekend in particular when I stayed in bed for two days because I simply could not face the world. My mother called, and after talking to me for a few minutes, she was ready to check me into a mental hospital for depression. I basically hung up on her, and my pity party continued for another few days. Finally, though, I got sick and tired of being sick and tired. I knew something had to change, and I decided to make it happen.

I started reading self-improvement books, and in one of them I discovered the quote "The definition of insanity is doing the same thing over and over and expecting different results." That was the smack in the head I needed. If I wanted something better in my life, I had to change my routine. This started my quest to lead a more well-rounded life. I began an exercise routine, hired a personal trainer, and started eating a healthy diet. After about six months, I shed my extra weight, which was a huge energy and confidence booster. I also improved my mental health by reading more positive books. My Sundays became a time to tend to my spirit instead of staying in bed.

My workdays shifted from being twelve-plus hours long to eight or nine hours long. My evenings were reserved for fun time and relaxing with friends and family. My work friends and I created a rule: the first one to bring up work had to buy the drinks for the evening. That was certainly an incentive to keep our conversations focused on other parts of our lives besides work! I also started a practice that I still make happen today: taking at least two fun vacations with family and friends each year.

When I started taking time to recharge my battery on a consistent basis, my productivity at work increased. As the saying goes, I got my groove back.

People Leadership Action Steps to Recharging Your Battery

1. Think about what you currently do to recharge your battery. Is it effective?

2. How can you do a better job of regenerating your energy? Create a plan of action for yourself.

3. Consider how having renewed energy every day might contribute to your success. What areas might you improve in if you had more energy?

4. Think of a leader you know who lives a well-rounded life. What do you admire most about him or her? What can you learn from him or her?

"Usually, when the distractions of daily life deplete our energy, the first thing we eliminate is the thing we need the most."

—Sarah Ban Breathnach

30
Be the Model

In late 2013, I was sitting in a lounge chair relaxing on the white sands of the panhandle of Florida when the screams and laughter of a group of children caused me to glance up from the novel I was reading. I discovered that they were skimboarding. (If you are not familiar with this sport, it involves throwing a small, thin surfboard-shaped board into the surf right at the edge of the shore where the water meets the sand, and then running and jumping on the board so you can glide along the shore for ten to twenty feet, depending on your skill level.) Most of the kids doing it were ten to fifteen years old. I watched for about ten minutes as some of the surfers glided elegantly and effortlessly across the shoreline while others watched and tried time and time again to mimic them.

Just as I was about to get back into my book, I saw out of the corner of my eye a new "skimmer" running excitedly to join the others. This little boy was probably about four or five years old. He ran up to the other surfers, and for about five minutes, he focused intently and watched the two boys who seemed more experienced than the rest of the group. Each time either of these boys took their turn skimboarding, not only were they successful, but they also added a few jumps and twists to their technique.

Apparently satisfied that he'd seen enough to try it out himself, the little boy started running, threw his skimboard down in the water, and jumped on. On this first attempt, he fell off into the water immediately. With no hesitation, he picked up his board, waited his turn, and tried again. And after I watched him try five or six times, I realized that, after each attempt, he was watching what the other kids were doing before he tried again. He was taking every one of his cues, whether it was technique or attitude, from the other kids. Because some of the kids were falling down and trying again, so was the he. Because some of the kids were trying to do a twist on their boards, so was he. I am sure the older kids had no clue as to the impact they were having on the little boy. Not once did they ever engage with him or give him instructions—yet he was watching, learning, and copying their actions and behaviors. They were this young boy's role models for the sport of skimboarding.

Just like that little boy watched those surfers in order to learn how to skimboard, your employees and team members are watching your every move to learn how they should perform in their roles. And just like those young surfers, you may not realize how much your employees are learning from your behaviors and leadership. Psychologists call this concept of watching and learning from others "mirroring" or "modeling." Most of the articles and writings about modeling discuss childrearing or working with children; however, my experience has shown me that regardless of our age, how we act is influenced by the actions of the people we see as leaders in our lives. As a people leader, it is important for you to model the behavior you want to see in your people. One of my favorite quotes comes from Mahatma Gandhi, who said, "Be the change you want to see in the world." I encourage all people leaders to "be the team member you want to see in your team."

You can be a good model for your team by:
- Setting equivalent standards.
- Letting your actions speak louder than your words.
- Showing your authentic passion and commitment to your work.

Set equivalent standards.

In early 2014, I was reading an article in *The Wall Street Journal* about parents teaching gratitude to their children. One sentence in particular in that article struck me as profoundly relevant to leading people: "You can't teach what you don't have," the author pointed out. And it's absolutely true: you can't expect of others what you aren't willing to do yourself. Remember Kenneth Lay and Jeffrey Skilling of Enron? Clearly they did not have personal integrity, so it should come as no surprise that some of the members of their team thought it was okay to defraud their financial picture.

Unfortunately, I have seen this kind of behavior all too often in my experience with CEOs, managers, supervisors, and team leaders. In working with leaders, I often discover that a disparity exists between the standards that they set for themselves and the standards they expect of their team members. When a leader asks his or her team members to behave or act in a certain manner and then turns around and operates in a completely different manner, it's obvious to everyone, especially his or her employees. A simple yet frequent example is when a leader expects his or her team to meet their deadlines on time and yet when the team asks their leader for something, he or she delivers it late. Another is when a leader asks his or her team members to not look at or use their smartphones or computers during a meeting, then spends the entire meeting looking at e-mails, taking phone calls, or responding to texts. These kinds of discordant behaviors do not lend themselves to a productive team environment.

When leaders vent to me about how frustrated they are with their employees' actions or behaviors, I often ask them how they would rate themselves in the same area. The reactions I get from the leaders is a telltale sign of their willingness to be the model for their team and to set equivalent standards. When they react to my question with indignation and anger that I had the nerve to question them in that way, I know I have a leader who is not a model for his or her team. If, however, the leaders respond with either quiet contemplation or recognition that my question has merit, then I know I can work with them to equalize the standards they set for themselves and their team members.

Effective people leaders understand the importance of equivalent standards and work to set them for themselves and their team members.

Actions speak louder than words.

Another critical element of serving as a good model for your team is doing what you say you will do. There are numerous so-called leaders who say one thing and do exactly the opposite. I don't know about you, but these kinds of leaders drive me nuts. People are motivated and inspired by leaders whose actions and words are aligned with each other—and personally, I prefer the leaders who are willing to let their actions speak louder than their words. These people are often labeled as being "quiet leaders," mostly because they are not showboaters. They set a vision, but they don't feel the need to talk about it; they just do it. Leaders like these deliver results on every level.

A great example of a company whose actions speak louder than their words is Southwest Airlines. Their in-flight magazine, *Southwest the Magazine,* contains a blurb in each edition from Gary Kelly—chairman, president, and CEO of Southwest Airlines—in which he shares amazing stories about how Southwest's employees have modeled excellent customer service. Every one I've read has been about a customer who encountered some sort of issue—his flight got cancelled, or she left her belonging on a plane, or his luggage was misplaced—and was helped by a Southwest employee.

In the December 2013 issue of the magazine, Mr. Kelly's entire article was about the heroic actions of his team. One story was about a customer who had lost his wallet. One of the pilots overheard him telling a flight attendant what had happened, and right on the spot he took action to help. Because the man didn't have a cell phone, the pilot let the man use his own phone to try to track down the missing wallet—and when he didn't find it, he gave him $40 of his own money so he could be comfortable for the rest of the trip. While the story wasn't covering modeling good behavior per se, I can only imagine that the flight attendant involved gained a lot of respect for that pilot and learned from his actions for future situations. Now that's what I call letting your actions speak louder than your words.

Show your passion and commitment to your work.

Now more than ever, people crave leaders who are passionate and committed to their work. I often hear people grumbling about how sick and tired they are of leaders and managers who simply show up for work, go through the motions in their roles, and have little to no passion or commitment to anyone or anything other than their own personal gain. Granted, it's hard to stay passionate and committed when you feel like the weight of the world is on your shoulders. It is easy to get burnt out and lose the love you once had for your work. However, being the model for your team requires you to dig deep and consistently demonstrate, day in and day out, your passion for and dedication to your job.

Showing your commitment and passion for your work means handling every task you perform, every encounter you engage in, and every problem you solve with an energy and expression that shows how much you care about the outcome—not just for yourself but also for the greater good. When your team members see that you enjoy what you're doing, that you are dedicated to what you're doing, and that you have a genuine desire to perform, your behavior will be contagious. Your passion will fuel others to be committed.

Commitment and dedication also means that you are willing to do what it takes—personally—to get the desired results. Leaders who are unwilling to get their hands dirty to help the business succeed do not demonstrate their commitment to the team. To be a model for your team, you must show that you are at least willing to lend a hand and be part of the solution if the need arises. It's crazy when leaders expect their teams to go above and beyond the call of duty, working long hours or even overtime to get the job done, when they themselves are nowhere to be found. Please don't misunderstand: I am not naively suggesting that leaders should perform mundane tasks on a frequent basis. However, I am suggesting that you demonstrate a willingness to contribute when you're needed.

If you want a team you can count on to deliver outstanding results, show them that you are passionate about your work and committed—both to your company and to them.

Being the Model in Action

It was the end of the sales year at Nortel, and there was a lot of pressure being applied—not only to the sales team but also to all of the other support teams—to meet the revenue goals of the business unit for the year. At the beginning of December, actual sales were significantly below target, and the executives of the division would not settle for less than that target—so the salespeople were working frantically and diligently with the customers, creating new proposals, closing new and existing deals, and ensuring that customers placed their orders in plenty of time for the products to ship prior to the end of the year.

The sales team's efforts were paying off—in the first two weeks of December, the order management team was receiving twice the number of orders they normally received each week. Unfortunately for everyone involved, especially the operations team, the orders had to be shipped by December 31 at 11:59 pm in order to be recognized as revenue. Phillip, the VP of operations, was receiving more calls than he knew what to do with, but the CEO wanted assurance that his team would get the orders entered and shipped in order to reach the revenue goals.

What Phillip wanted to do was chastise the sales team for waiting until the last month of the year to drum up so much new business, but instead he bit his tongue, expressed confidence in his team, and assured the executives that his team would put in a Herculean effort to get the orders shipped. Then he reached out to two of his key directors—Lydia, the director of order management, and Geoffrey, the director of shipping—to strategize about how to meet the challenge ahead.

After assessing their options, Lydia and Geoffrey agreed that they needed as many people as possible to help receive incoming products; enter new orders; and pick, pack, and ship product—which meant that they needed Phillip's entire staff to help out with the task at hand, and they needed Phillip to approve overtime for anyone willing to put in the extra time. Phillip quickly agreed to their requests, and he engaged his broader group by asking for volunteers from teams whose year-end commitments were not as pressing.

The day after Phillip began to rally the troops, Lydia visited the order management workspace to see how her team was progressing. She was surprised to find Phillip sitting at a desk attempting to enter a customer order into the order management system. The order management representatives in the area told Lydia that Phillip had been there first thing that morning asking what he could do to help. When Lydia told Phillip that he did not need to enter orders, he said he wanted everyone to know he was committed to meeting their goals of getting the orders entered no matter what it took. It was obvious to Lydia that Phillip was not an expert at order entry—in fact, he was actually slowing down the process—but she quickly saw that his commitment to help was energizing the team and motivating them to work harder, so she let him continue.

After a couple hours of order entry, Phillip ventured across town to the warehouse to see how they were progressing there. When he got there, it was chaos. Semitrailers were backed up in the parking lot, waiting to deliver incoming product to fulfill the orders, and there were hundreds of other orders ready to be picked up. The packing lines looked like Santa's workshop on Christmas Eve, with boxes piled high waiting to be shipped out the door.

Phillip had started his career out as a warehouse worker, so he knew he could help out this team. He went to Geoffrey, said he was ready to pick some orders, and asked how he could get started. Geoffrey was shocked at Phillip's offer and was tempted to decline—however, he sensed that it would be good for his team to see Phillip, the VP of operations, in the trenches and sharing the workload with them, so he gave him something to do. Things went much better than they had in order management; Phillip was fairly successful at picking orders, and he helped the warehouse team tremendously.

This high-pressure activity lasted for the entire second half of December. During this time period, Phillip remained optimistic and energetic and was always present to lend a helping hand and to show his support for the team. Phillip was being the model employee that he wanted all his team members to be. His dedication, passion, and commitment to meet the year-end demands made the operations team work harder to achieve their goals, and it improved their overall attitude; even under intense pressure and stress, in fact, there was a sense of camaraderie and strength throughout the organization for those two weeks.

At 11:59 pm on December 31, the team's efforts paid off. They had shipped every order that was placed, and the division not only met their expected revenue targets—they exceeded them.

People Leadership Action Steps to Being the Model

1. If I asked you to take an inventory of the standards you have for yourself at work and those you have for your team, would they be equivalent? If so, how so? If not, reflect upon how they are misaligned and what can you do to align them.

2. Think of a situation at work when your actions did not match up with your words. How did that make you feel? What impact did your actions have on your team?

3. Take a moment to think about your levels of passion and commitment for your role. Are they strong? If not, what can you do to ignite your passion and commitment to your work?

4. Think about a leader who you admire because he or she serves as a stellar model for his or her team. What does he or she do? What do you admire most about him or her?

"Nothing so conclusively proves a man's ability to lead others as what he does from day to day to lead himself."

—Thomas J. Watson

Leadership Lessons from My 10-year-old Niece

To be a leader you be nice to friends and solve problems. Most people are leaders, some are not. To be a leader you have to be nice and be able to solve problems. Leaders are kind to everyone including mean people. I hope you become a leader just like I do!

By Sofia Rose Faust

Acknowledgments

This book has been a long time in the making, and it would not have been possible without some very important people who helped along the way. Mom, you were with me every step of the way, from idea to crappy first draft to my final version. Thanks for always being available to offer input, direction, and most importantly the belief that I would actually complete my work. Dad, thank you for offering your pearls of wisdom about people and life in our conversations. I love both of you so much, and I am grateful every day that I have such amazing parents!

To Carrie, Russell, Annette, and Elizabeth, my initial proofreaders of what I thought was a final version: your effort to read the book and provide your heartfelt insight and opinions was invaluable to me.

To Brooke, my writing coach: If I had not been introduced to you, this book would still be a draft on my computer, never to be seen by the reading public. Your teachings, edits, and encouragements are what really made this possible.

To the team at She Write Press: thank you for allowing me to be a part of your portfolio and for leading me through the publishing process.

To Kevin, my beloved partner: Thanks so much for supporting me through this process. It was not easy, and I know I had my moments—but you were always there to encourage me to keep moving on. I love you!

And last and certainly not least, to all the leaders and mentors throughout my personal and professional life who shaped me into the leader I am today: you know who you are, and I cannot thank you enough for telling me that I was smart and capable and for allowing me to take risks, to make mistakes, and to learn and move forward to be a better and stronger person. Also, I want to thank everyone who was ever a part of one of my teams or organizations. I learned from each and every one of you in our interactions, positive or negative. This book would not exist without you, and I thank you for your part in the story.

About the Author

© James Ostrand

Gina Folk is a dynamic and inspirational leader of people, process, and change. She has more than twenty years of experience helping organizations and individuals to achieve outstanding performance results, and she has led global organizations and change efforts that have delivered improvements valued in the tens of millions of dollars. Her passion and talent to help others meet their full potential is displayed in the numerous leadership and excellence awards she received in her tenure at a large Fortune 500 company.

Folk left her senior management role in corporate America in 2010 to pursue a speaking, writing, and consulting career. She currently works with companies of all sizes to train and mentor their direct line managers and supervisors, empowering them to become effective people leaders.

Folk holds an MBA from Belmont University and a BS in psychology and business from Vanderbilt University, and she is a certified Lean Six Sigma Black Belt.

Folk offers a series of services for companies and individuals who have a need and desire to improve the skills and effectiveness of their people leaders. From group training classes to speaking engagements to one-on-one guidance and coaching for supervisors, management, and executives, Folk's expertise is guaranteed to deliver positive results in your organization.

If you are ready to get started improving people leadership skills in your organization, contact Gina Folk now at (727) 482-0782, or visit her website, www.peopleleadership.com.

SELECTED TITLES FROM SHE WRITES PRESS

She Writes Press is an independent publishing company
founded to serve women writers everywhere.
Visit us at www.shewritespress.com.

The Thriver's Edge: Seven Keys to Transform the Way You Live, Love, and Lead
by Donna Stoneham $16.95, 978-1-63152-980-1
A "coach in a book" from master executive coach and leadership expert Dr. Donna
Stoneham, *The Thriver's Edge* outlines a practical road map to breaking free of the
barriers keeping you from being everything you're capable of being.

Think Better. Live Better. 5 Steps to Create the Life You Deserve by Francine Huss
$16.95, 978-1-938314-66-7
With the help of this guide, readers will learn to cultivate more creative thoughts,
realign their mindset, and gain a new perspective on life.

*Stop Giving it Away: How to Stop Self-Sacrificing and Start Claiming Your Space,
Power, and Happiness* by Cherilynn Veland $16.95, 978-1-63152-958-0
An empowering guide designed to help women break free from the trappings of the
needs, wants, and whims of other people—and the self-imposed limitations that
are keeping them from happiness.

100 Under $100: One Hundred Tools for Empowering Global Women by Betsy Teutsch
$29.95, 978-1-63152-934-4
An inspiring, comprehensive look at the many tools being employed today to
empower women in the developing world and help them raise themselves out of
poverty.

The Great Healthy Yard Project: Our Yards, Our Children, Our Responsibility by
Diane Lewis, MD $24.95, 978-1-938314-86-5
A comprehensive look at the ways in which we are polluting our drinking water
and how it's putting our children's future at risk—and what we can do to turn
things around.

The Complete Enneagram: 27 Paths to Greater Self-Knowledge by Beatrice Chestnut, PhD
$24.95, 978-1-938314-54-4
A comprehensive handbook on using the Enneagram to do the self-work required
to reach a higher stage of personal development.

CPSIA information can be obtained
at www.ICGtesting.com
Printed in the USA
FSOW02n0858171114
3492FS